Everything Originated from Milk

Case Study of Nestlé

Everything Originated from Milk

Case Study of Nestlé

Hiroo Takahashi

Hakuoh University, Japan

World Scientific

NEW JERSEY · LONDON · SINGAPORE · BEIJING · SHANGHAI · HONG KONG · TAIPEI · CHENNAI · TOKYO

Published by

World Scientific Publishing Co. Pte. Ltd.

5 Toh Tuck Link, Singapore 596224

USA office: 27 Warren Street, Suite 401-402, Hackensack, NJ 07601

UK office: 57 Shelton Street, Covent Garden, London WC2H 9HE

Library of Congress Cataloging-in-Publication Data
Names: Takahashi, Hiroo, 1944–   author.
Title: Everything originated from milk : case study of Nestlé /
    Hiroo Takahashi, Hakuoh University, Japan.
Description: Singapore ; Hackensack, NJ : World Scientific Publishing Co. Pte Ltd., [2021] |
    Includes bibliographical references.
Identifiers: LCCN 2021013943 | ISBN 9789811234088 (hardcover) | ISBN 9789811235917 (ebook)
Subjects: LCSH: Nestlé. | Food industry and trade--Switzerland--Case studies.
Classification: LCC HD9015.S94 N478 2021 | DDC 338.7/664009494--dc22
LC record available at https://lccn.loc.gov/2021013943

British Library Cataloguing-in-Publication Data
A catalogue record for this book is available from the British Library.

For any available supplementary material, please visit
https://www.worldscientific.com/worldscibooks/10.1142/12202#t=suppl

Desk Editor: Lum Pui Yee

Typeset by Stallion Press
Email: enquiries@stallionpress.com

Contents

Acknowledgments

The successful publication of this book is the result of many scholars' efforts in the fields of international management and business ethics, and of the work of institutions such as the Academy of International Business (AIB, based in the US), the Academy of Multinational Enterprises (AME, based in Japan), the Japan Academy of International Business (JAIB), and the Japan Society for Business Ethics (JABES).

I am very grateful to have been given the chance to be a visiting professor at the Lubin School of Business, Pace University, New York; Southern Taiwan University of Science and Technology, Taiwan; NIDA Business School, Thammasat Business School, Thailand; Atma Jaya Business School, Indonesia; Sofia University, Bulgaria; Renmin University of China, Beijing; Ritsumeikan Asia Pacific University, Japan.

My greatest support for this publication comes from interviews and support given by Mr. Michael Briner, Zone AOA (Asia, Oceania and sub-Saharan Africa) Group, Vice President; Mr. Chris Hogg, Zone AOA, Head of Corporate Communication; Ms. Claude Schwitiz, AOA, Head of Corporate Communication; Ms. Yao Yang, AOA, Beverage Strategic Business Unit; Mr. Andrew-Hartford Smith, Director, Corporate Training & Learning of Nestlé Corporate Headquarters, Vevey, Switzerland; and Mr. Kozo Takaoka, President; Ms. Miki Kano, Executive Officer, Corporate Communication; Mr. Yuji Serizawa, Executive Officer, Human Resource; Mr. Makoto Nakaoka, Executive Officer, Marketing Management of Nestlé Japan, Kobe, Japan.

I am also grateful to the support provided by Mr. Itaru Nagano as professional translator, Mr. Max Phua, Managing Director and Ms. Lum Pui Yee, Senior Editor of World Scientific Publishing Co., Singapore.

Preface

It All Started with A Drop of Milk

When we hear the company name 'Nestlé,' we think of it as a synonym for instant coffee. For the younger generation, it would be associated with Kit Kat chocolates. However, Nestlé is actually a large global corporation handling a wide variety of food products reaching all corners of the globe. Many people call it a food giant. Nestle has made inroads into Japan over the last hundred years, and it has been assimilated into the Japanese society as if it is a native enterprise.

Nestlé is originally a Swiss company, but most of its products are sold outside its homeland. Although Switzerland is a small country in Europe, it has many global corporations that thrive all over the world, besides Nestlé. How can a company, born in a country of mountains and lakes without natural resources, become such a vast global corporation? Nestlé is the best example that answers this question. Food is basically a domestic entity that is rooted in a specific country. How could a company such as Nestlé grow into a world reigning super global corporation? This book aims to clarify the entire answer behind this question to the best of my ability and to try to draw up guidelines for Japanese global corporations.

It was about half a century ago that I became interested in Nestlé. While studying in the United States, I visited Switzerland and dropped by the town of Vevey which is close to Lausanne, home of the International Olympic Committee. It was then that I came across Nestlé. At that time, I was just looking at an elegant building standing gloriously beside Lake Leman, without any idea that it was a leading global corporation nestled at the very place I was standing. A few years after that experience, I had an opportunity to join a research project in which Japanese senior company executives visited European and American multinational corporations. The first company we chose for our visit in Europe as a typical multinational company was Nestlé. I had exceptionally fond memories of my earlier visit while I was listening to the presentations given by Nestle's executives, and later as I looked down from the conference room at Lake Leman. They also took us on a tour of their chocolate factory in the hills. In those days, most Japanese just associated Nestlé with instant coffee. It was the first time for me to realize that the company handled chocolates as well.

We were further informed that IMEDE (Institut pour l'Etude des Methodes de Direction de l'Entreprise), co-established with Harvard Business School, was in Lausanne and we decided to visit it the next day. Nestlé was devoting much effort to human resource development since its early days, so they established such a business school. IMEDE later merged with Centre d'Etudes Industrielles (CEI) in Geneva to become IMD (International Institute for Management Development) which became a leading business school in Europe.

These experiences, first about a half century ago, next at IMEDE, and several visits thereafter, prompted me to compile a comprehensive picture of Nestlé. However, my full-time university position kept me from having enough time to study it deeply. A few years ago, I was freed from that situation and I could concentrate on the work. I started to collect materials on Nestlé, made a new visit to the Nestlé Headquarters in Vevey, and conducted an interview survey at Nestlé Japan in Kobe. The scope of Nestlé is enormously broad and their management activities are changing from moment to moment. Even while writing this book, I continued to receive new news releases from the Nestlé Public Relations section.

In this book, I would like to touch on issues such as the following:

1. Nestlé's roots.
2. Nestlé's current business situation.
3. M&A as a development strategy.
4. Nestlé's global research and development network.
5. CSV management efforts as Nestlé's strategic target.
6. Nestlé's human resources development system.
7. Switzerland as the birthplace of Nestlé.

I must however admit, even after all my research, that it is quite difficult even for Nestlé's employees to visualize the entire scale of Nestlé in detail. To do so, one must consider the company's sales bases in as many as 189 countries, production factories in 413 places, research and development bases in 41 places, with more than 1,000 brands. I have, as mentioned above, tried to even explore part of Nestlé's ever-changing management situation. If, however, should there be any misinterpretations or statistical errors in the current Nestlé management, all responsibilities lie with me. I welcome any candid comments from readers.

Takahashi

About the Author

Hiroo Takahashi is Professor Emeritus of International Management and Business Ethics in the Graduate School of Business at Hakuoh University, Japan. He was a visiting scholar at Stern School of Business, New York University (1971–73), Visiting Professor at Rubin School of Business, Pace University, New York (2003–4), Visiting Professor of NIDA Business School, Thailand (2016–), Sofia University, Bulgaria (2016–) and Southern Taiwan University of Science & Technology (2010–18). He was also a director at the Business Research Institute in Tokyo.

He obtained his Ph.D Degree at Chuo University, Tokyo.

Prof Takahashi specializes in Organization Structure, R&D strategy and Business Ethics of Global Corporations. He has done field studies of over 200 Multinational Companies such as Nestle, 3M, Johnson & Johnson, IBM, Xerox and Japanese Multinationals in the past thirty years. Dr Takahashi has published numerous articles and books such as "Organization Strategy of Global Management", "Global Management of R&D", "Ethics Code of Global Business" and "Leadership of Global Business". He published a new book with the title "Modern International Management Strategy" in 2011, "The Challenge for Japanese Multinationals" in 2013 with Palgrave Macmillan, England, "Business Ethics as Strategy" in 2016, with Maruzen, "Everything originated from Milk — Case of Nestle" (Japanese Version) with Dobunkan Publishing in 2019.

Chapter 1

The Birth of Nestlé, A Global Corporation

1. Nestlé's Birth at Vevey, Switzerland

When we hear the company name 'Nestlé,' most of us would see the images of 'Nestlé Instant Coffee' and 'Nescafé Gold Blend Coffee' in our minds. As such, Nestlé is a very familiar part of our lives through its products and advertising. Even though we know the brand names of the products around us, many of us don't know much about the companies that produce them. The producers are usually known to us by their brand names rather than their company names. If you say Kit Kat, any chocolate lover will immediately tell you it is chocolate, but not many people know that it is a Nestlé product. Likewise, people are not too interested to know where the Nestlé company is nestled. People tend to consider familiar brands to be made by companies of their own country, like Sony, Toyota, etc. The world's well-known global corporations consider the wide-spreading of their brands to be their ultimate management goal. After all, although a company has its own birthplace, that doesn't matter so much if its brands have spread to many parts of the world and come to be loved by local consumers. Whoever its real country is, its foster parents are its clients and consumers. That is the corporate strategy that global corporations are aiming at. If a global corporation conducts business overseas and contributes to the economic growth of the local countries, it is a good thing for the development of both. That is to say, a win-win relationship is the corporate strategy that a global corporation should aim at.

It was about 100 years ago that Nestlé entered the Japanese market. Therefore, many people in Japan should be familiar with its products. When Nestlé first entered the Japanese market, it sold powdered milk solely for infants, thus very few people knew the company name of Nestlé. What made Nestlé spectacularly famous was its instant coffee, which made debut as a popular item post World War II. All one had to do was to pour hot water over the coffee powder to enjoy a steaming Western-style drink. Nestlé's instant coffee gained instant popularity in the Japanese market.

Where was this instant-coffee-maker Nestlé born? Nestlé has bases in nearly 189 countries, a number that is almost the same as the number of UN member countries. Since food products are so closely related to our daily lives, any place where people live can be its market. Even so, it is difficult to find a global company so assimilated into practically every corner of the globe as Nestlé.

If you look closely at Nestlé's products, you'll find the indication 'Vevey Switzerland.' (Please refer to Figure 1-1.) Nestlé, without any question, was born in the town of Vevey, Switzerland. Until today, Vevey is still Nestlé's gateway to the world, as this is where Nestlé's

Figure 1-1 The Birthplace of Nestlé: Vevey, Switzerland

headquarters nestles. Vevey is a small resort town along Switzerland's Lake Geneva, about an hour's train ride from the international city of Geneva. Among Vevey's neighboring towns are Lausanne (where the International Olympic Committee is head-quartered) and Montreux (famous for its Montreux Jazz Festival). The latter is also famous for its medieval castle on the bank of Lake Geneva. Switzerland is filled with picturesque sights wherever you go, but above all, Geneva, Lausanne, Vevey and Montreux are espe-cially romantic and attractive, because all of them lie among moun-tains and lakes.

What is it that has made Nestlé, born in the small town of Vevey, a world-reigning super global corporation? Basically, most global corporations first develop themselves in the countries of their origins, and then try to expand themselves on the interna-tional stage with strong footings within their own countries. In that sense, for a company to evolve towards the international market, ample management experiences within its own country are required. Most of the European, American and Japanese advanced companies progressed to the international market based on their management experiences within their own countries. In particular, is Switzerland, where Nestlé was born, large enough as a market? In terms of geographical area, it is just a little larger than Kyushu, Japan. In terms of population, it is approximately 8.5 million cur-rently, but it was only 2 million or so at the time when Nestlé's founder Henri Nestlé was born.

Does Switzerland naturally have a solid economic foundation with raw materials required for business development? Wherever you go in Switzerland, you would see lofty mountains, lakes of vari-ous sizes and shapes, towns here and there and cottage-style houses among them. These sights are now precious tourist resources, but it was not so in the past. Switzerland lies among lofty mountains with limited farmland and mineral resources. But the Swiss successfully turned these disadvantages into their advan-tages by developing their tourist resources and economic infra-structure to make the present Switzerland.

Coincidentally, Japan shares this same situation with Switzerland. What were the primary factors behind the economic development achieved by Japan, a small island country? It was Japanese wisdom and a drive to turn disadvantages into advantages, by rising to these challenges with human intelligence and the fruits of innovation (in today's parlance). Today, many Swiss companies are reigning the world as global corporations beyond their domestic market, and Nestlé is the most representative and symbolic company among them. These global corporations are the supporters of Switzerland's strong economic infrastructure, propelling Switzerland to the top positions in various global competitiveness ranking surveys. This fact underscores the efficacy of the above-mentioned factors. (Please refer to Chapter 7.)

2. Everything Originated from Milk

Take a train from Vevey, ride for about an hour among mountains, then change to a mountain train to arrive at the village of Gruyères on top of a hill. It is the home of the world-famous Gruyères cheese. Cheese-making still flourishes among neighboring villages, which are the spots where tourists can actually observe the cheese-making process. What is a typical Swiss food? The answer should invariably be 'cheese.' Cheese is such an indispensable item in their daily lives. In fact, the food representative of Switzerland is cheese fondue. Cheese fondue is a simple dish as it is just a pot of melted cheese and eaten with bread. It is one of Switzerland's national foods. Tourists to Switzerland would likely try cheese fondue at least once to enjoy the feeling of actually being in Switzerland.

Since cheese is made from cow's milk, large tracts of pastureland are required for cattle grazing. In Japan, Hokkaido, with its vast pastureland, is most suited to raise livestock and hence for dairy business to be developed there. The climate of Switzerland is similar to that of Hokkaido, but it is short of flat pastureland. Thus, Swiss raised their livestock by utilizing hill slopes for pastureland. Switzerland is not blessed with large farmlands to grow agricultural products. So, they almost solely depended on livestock for their food supply. Getting milk by raising cows and making the best use of it was the way to sustain their living. Till now, you can still catch a glimpse of grazing cattle among mountains a short distance away from tourist spots. However, they do not look like age-old farming villages. These scenes, peculiar to Switzerland, matches well with cottage-style houses. They are actually tourism resources intended to please the eyes of travelers. In order to preserve such scenes, quite a lot of implementation effort is required, for which financial support is provided by the government. From here we can see Switzerland's toughness and shrewdness, and that much energy has been put in to preserve these sights.

I once took a two-week tour of the United Kingdom. There, you don't see lofty mountains as in Switzerland. Instead, you see gently sloping ranges of hills. As with Japan, the UK is an island country and its altitude is a little higher than that of Hokkaido, but they rarely have heavy snow because of its position along the meeting of warm and cold sea currents. Weather fluctuations there are so great that you may sometimes experience all the four seasons even within one day. It may have been raining an hour ago, but the sun may be shining in a cloudless sky now. The temperature there is not too high and not too low throughout the year, which makes it suitable for plant growth. Grass grows naturally there. The world-famous English gardens, called 'flower artwork,' are nurtured in such climatic and natural features. In Japan, its countryside is mostly farmland. But in the UK where rice is not its people's staple food, they have turned their grass fields on gently sloping hillsides into grazing meadows for sheep. Sheep provide wool for the textile industry. Wherever you go in the UK, you'll find sheep freely grazing the Green Green Grass (as in the hit song 'Green Green Grass of Home' of the 1960s, sung by Japan's Ryoko Moriyama).

Sheep eat grass and excrete, and their excrement, in turn, becomes enriched soil for the grass to grow. This age-old ecosystem in the UK is most suited for sheep rearing and resulted in the increased number of sheep. People racked their brains to find a way to efficiently produce wool products, which led to the development of the textile industry. Triggered by this development, a variety of machinery were invented, which led to the Industrial Revolution. Countries such as Switzerland, the United Kingdom and Japan have built their industrial infrastructure making the best use of natural resources they have.

Cows can also be used as food, such as beef steak. In Switzerland, however, cows have supplied milk to make a variety of dairy products. Whenever we think of dairy products, the things that come to our minds would be butter, cheese and milk. Milk is highly nutritious and so it is most suitable as a source of nutrients for infants. Considering that babies can grow on cow's milk, without the need for human's breast milk, we can see how high its nutritional value is.

Further up in the mountains from Gruyères, you'll find a Nestlé chocolate factory. I once visited the factory. Initially, it was not a Nestlé factory. Nestlé acquired, on a merger and acquisition (M&A) basis, a company called Cailler that had introduced the world's first milk chocolate to the market. (This factory is called Maison Cailler, and its Visitor Center is open for tours.) Cailler added milk to cacao beans to make highly nutritious milk chocolate and spread it to the world. This is one of the discoveries that made Switzerland the pioneer in making use of milk. Now, when we speak of Switzerland, we immediately associate it with chocolate. Wherever you go in Switzerland, you'll find various and sundry chocolates all around the country. Chocolate is one of the first merchandise items bought by most tourists while in Switzerland.

3. The Challenge Faced by Henri Nestlé, the Founder

The establishment of the company Nestlé is nonetheless unrelated to milk. Milk is now commercialized as a variety of processed goods, and Nestlé is a pioneer in commercializing these processed goods. The name of the company comes from its founder Henri Nestlé. (Please refer to Figure 1-2.) Henri Nestlé was a German

Figure 1-2   Henri Nestlé, the Founder

born in Frankfurt am Main. His name in German was Heinrich Nestle, and the family name *Nestle* means 'a little nest' in German. It was later changed to the French spelling *Nestlé*. The Nestlé's logo is just literally 'a bird's nest,' representing a lovely mother feeding her infants. (Please refer to Figure 1-1.) Many Nestlé family ancestors were glaziers by profession. Henri Nestlé's father was also a glazier and made window panes, glass bottles, etc. He also handled English crockery.

At the age of 15 or so, Henri Nestlé started working as an apprentice at a pharmacy in Frankfurt. In those days, Germany was having conflicts with neighboring countries and the country was in an unstable condition. Thus, he fled to Vevey from Germany where he was born and raised until the age of 29. At that time, Switzerland had already established a system of permanent neutrality, and kept a neutral position as opposed to neighboring countries. Nestlé, after arriving at the politically stable country, began to work at a pharmacy in Vevey by making use of his experience as a pharmacist apprentice in Germany. Besides selling medicines, Nestlé also engaged himself in the business of manufacturing and selling of mineral water, carbonated lemonade, oil, vinegar, mustard, etc. It was said that he also manufactured and sold liquified gas cylinders for gas-lights, cement, concrete block materials, etc.

Curiosity-minded Nestlé involved himself in the business of manufacturing and selling of a variety of merchandise. What caught his attention in his busy days in Switzerland was that a number of infants died shortly after birth. This phenomenon was a serious social problem in other countries such as Germany and France as well. In some countries in Europe, 15 to 20 percent of infants died within one year of birth. Particularly, many female factory workers lost their children to malnutrition as they were unable to breastfeed their infants. Nestlé's siblings were no exception. His earnest desire to save infants' lives prompted him to make use of nutrition-rich milk. Nestlé's father-in-law was a medical doctor. His wife, Anna Clémentine Thérèse Ehemant, influenced by her doctor father, was said to have given various pieces of medical advice to Nestlé.

Very likely, this idea of making use of milk wouldn't have occurred to Nestlé if he had not moved to Switzerland. Freshness is most important to raw milk, but it doesn't keep long. In order to make cow milk preservable and more accessible to mothers, Nestlé made baby food out of milk paste containing concentrated milk and sugar only. Nestlé later on, through trial and error, developed infant cereal by mixing wheat with milk. Once, thinned cereal was given to a premature baby who was unable to take any food and on the verge of death. The baby headed for recovery in just a few days. This story spread rapidly around the neighboring villages as a 'miracle nutrition,' particularly among mothers with infants. This infant-saving cereal spread to nearby countries as well, paving a way for Nestlé to get much attention. Nestlé, in his later days, talked about this cereal. He said: "I didn't particularly discover something new, but I compounded long-known materials in a rational manner to make the best possible nutrients for infants." He also said that the main ingredients were just the best possible Swiss milk, bread and sugar.

Nestlé developed this baby food at the age of 54, twenty-four years after he came to Vevey. Nestlé referred to this product in a modest way, but it must not be forgotten that this is really a great invention achieved by spending a long period of time in development and manufacturing.

4. Nestlé's Merger with the Anglo-Swiss Condensed Milk Company and Its 2nd Establishment

In line with the increasing sales of baby food, Nestlé expanded the Vevey factory and was manufacturing 2,000 cans of baby food per day with 20 employees at work. At that time in 1872, Henri Nestlé was 58. The company began to export the baby food not only to European countries but also to children's hospitals in the US, Australia, South America, etc. It too was highly valued in those countries and the sales grew rapidly.

In order to keep up with this growth in sales, it became necessary to build a new and large modern factory. (Please refer to Figure 1-3.) However, at that time, Henri Nestlé was already over 60 and was not so ambitious to expand his factory on his own. So, in 1875, he sold his factory in Vevey to a Swiss financial group along with the brand name of Nestlé. From these facts, we can assume that Henri Nestlé might have been more suitable as a researcher or scientist than a businessman.

Figure 1-3   Nestlé Factory in Vevey, Switzerland (1890)

In 1877, two years after Henri Nestlé sold his company to the financial group, the Anglo Swiss Condensed Milk Company started selling condensed milk by imitating Nestlé's. Anglo Swiss was founded by two brothers Charles and George Page, and was operating extensively in the United States. Before long, they caught wind of the abundant supply of milk in Switzerland. The brothers made inroads there and started their milk-related business. Anglo Swiss, already with factories in 15 places within the United States, began to expand to the UK, Germany and Switzerland.

With the entry of Anglo Swiss into Switzerland, fierce competition erupted between the two companies in their condensed milk business. Anglo Swiss was much larger, both in capital and scale, for Nestlé to compete with. However, Anglo Swiss faced its own management crisis due to the building of factories and business expansion in the United States. On the other hand, Borden, famed for its Lady Borden ice cream, entered into the condensed milk market, and the competition between the two companies became fiercer. Anglo Swiss finally had to sell some of its US factories to Borden. Borden, Inc. was founded by Gail Borden and achieved great success in the manufacturing of canned condensed milk. Since canned milk was handy to carry about, highly nutritious and preservable, it gained great popularity in the urban areas where milk was scarce. It was also highly sought-after in California which was then in a red-hot gold rush boom. American condensed milk businesses experienced even fiercer competition as they expanded to Switzerland. Anglo Swiss, which had already taken root in Switzerland, eventually achieved recovery by merging with Nestlé.

Anglo Swiss succeeded Nestlé's brands in the form of M&A by Nestlé. (Please refer to Figure 1-4.) Nestlé founded his company in 1867, the Page brothers founded their company in 1866, and these two companies merged and started a new company in 1905. Thus, Nestlé acquired a foothold to expand into the American market as well as the European market.

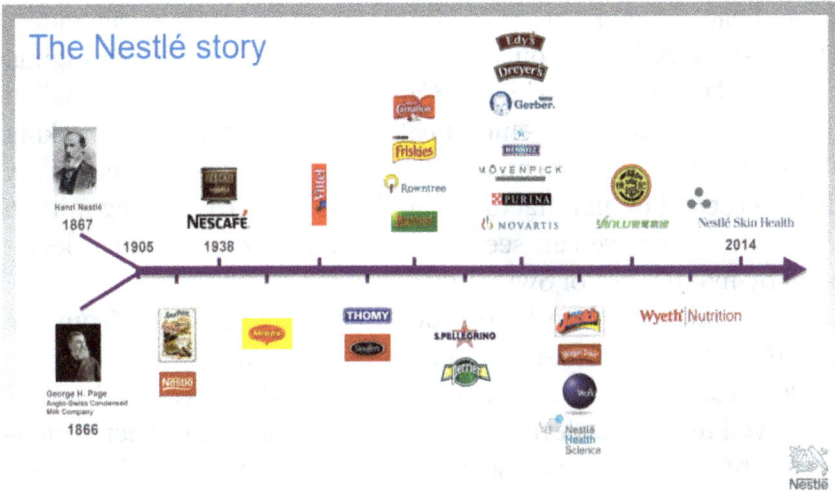

Figure 1-4   A Summary of Nestlé's History

5. Adoption of the Chocolate Business

The unexpected merger with an American company paved the foundation for Nestlé to acquire management skills. That is, M&A, if handled properly, can become the driving force for a corporate strategy. When we talk about Nestlé's development, we are reminded of its history of mergers and acquisitions, in which Nestlé made the first achievement of making a great leap by merging with the American company. The merger of the two companies made it possible for them to make a breakthrough beyond Switzerland into the American market.

What made Nestlé achieve further development was the entry into the chocolate industry. In those days, chocolate was sold in pharmacies in the category of expensive medicine. Thus, chocolate must have been of interest to Nestlé as much as condensed milk. Chocolate was already on the market when Nestlé was born in 1814. In 1819, Francois Louis Cailler first started to manufacture chocolate. Chocolate production was not yet automated then, thus chocolate was made by kneading using water power. To make chocolate, ground cacao beans was made into a paste and sugar was added. The paste was cooled outdoors before being cut for packaging. Later on, Daniel Peter, who was Cailler's son-in-law and also hailed from Vevey, made some modifications and succeeded in making chocolate in a more chemical way. Cailler was the first company that succeeded in manufacturing milk chocolate (by adding milk to chocolate). Here we can see another example of a product developed by making use of Swiss milk.

The milk chocolate Callier developed was different from the 'cacao sugar candy' that Anglo Swiss had so far been selling. He made cacao into powder through a chemical process and added preserved milk to it. Vevey-born Peter, who must have been watching Nestlé's advancement, succeeded in developing the milk chocolate on his own as he had kept up his chocolate/milk mixture experiments.

Callier's milk chocolate is now sold under the brand name of Nestlé. Another chocolate brand widely seen in Switzerland is Lindt. It was developed by Rudolphe Lindt, a pharmacist in Bern, the de-facto capital of Switzerland. It melts gently in your mouth and is called 'fondant chocolate.' It became very popular as soon as it was put on the market. The production technology of this melt-in-the-mouth chocolate was referred to as an epoch-making discovery at that time.

The production methods developed by Callier and Lindt expanded not only into continental Europe but also to the United Kingdom. Thus, chocolate became a familiar food for the people and its demand increased rapidly. Particularly in Switzerland, many companies large and small began making chocolates, thereby causing excessive competition. As a result, chocolate companies experienced a downturn and some even lost their businesses. Callier was no exception. Under such circumstances, it tried to maintain its chocolate business by merging with Nestlé. Nestlé on its part was then able to advance further with chocolate as one of its major fields. After this, Nestlé took over the well-established English chocolate brand Kit Kat to make its chocolate business unshakable.

6. What Nestlé Learned During Its Startup Period

Supposing that the period from the middle to the end of 1800s was the period of Nestlé's birth and development, and the period after 1905 of its merger with Anglo Swiss was the period of its re-start, Nestlé's subsequent development can be considered the expansion of its business sphere and the incorporation of overseas markets, with its business expansion mostly owed to the acquisition of external resources through M&A.

During the 1900s, Nestlé continued to acquire companies such as Maggi (well-known for its pre-mixed soups in Switzerland), German and French ice cream companies, a French yogurt company, frozen food and canned food companies in America, a French company dealing in water, etc.

However, the instant coffee, which helped Nestlé achieve an unassailable position, was developed originally by Nestlé. In the late 1920s, the bumper crop of coffee beans in Brazil caused a sharp price drop. The Brazilian government, struggling to find a breakthrough in the situation, asked Nestlé to find an outlet for the overproduced coffee beans. After several years of development, Nestlé put on the market its original merchandise under the brand of 'Nescafé®.' It was powdered coffee, and all one had to do was just pour hot water to it. It was also convenient to carry around. So, it became an instant hit among households, and it particularly became a necessity for soldiers fighting in the war. Switzerland, a permanently neutral nation, was not involved in any full-scale war, but the demand for food products was large among warring nations. Thus, the instant coffee business helped the Swiss economy to grow. Nestlé's principal products in its early days such as condensed milk, chocolate, soup and coffee became soldiers' necessities, helping the company to achieve further growth. Coffee entered Japan with the US forces which was stationed there after World War II and became popular among general households.

From what we have observed so far, it is evident that Nestlé's expansion was achieved through its international relations rather than domestic relations. Since Switzerland is a small country, Swiss companies had to look into the possibility of expanding into international markets. The question is why they could achieve such success. Nestlé's traditional management method was to secure M&A deals with overseas companies and to incorporate international markets. This method has continued to the present. We need to understand that such features of Swiss companies are deeply related to the history of the nation's foundation. (Please refer to Chapter 7.)

7. Relations of Swiss companies with the Outside World

Switzerland is surrounded by France, Germany and Italy, and has been built under the influences of these countries. This reality is clearly seen from the fact that they still use the languages of the three nations as official languages. French is spoken around Geneva, which is close to the French border. German is spoken around Zurich, which is close to the German border. Italian is spoken around Lugano, which is close to the Italian border. It should be remembered that such a geographical location of Switzerland is the greatest factor in discussing its cultural and historical positions. Switzerland, surrounded by lofty mountains and short of mineral resources and farmland, had to earn its living by trading with neighboring countries. That is to say, crossing national borders was nothing out of the ordinary for the Swiss.

Another factor from which the Swiss cannot escape is that they were always exposed to conflicts among the neighboring countries because of the geographical position. During the 19th century, civil wars and conflicts were constantly occurring among neighboring European countries like France, Germany, Italy, etc., while Switzerland maintained a neutral stance, impartial towards any of those countries. Consequently, quite a few people fled to Switzerland as asylum seekers. Switzerland thus developed itself in these adverse circumstances where many in the population were immigrants from abroad. The situation is still true even today. The population of Switzerland is approximately 8.5 million, of which more than 2 million are of foreign descent. The percentage of the latter to the total population is extremely high compared to other countries of the world. To name just a few of them, Henri Nestlé, the founder of Nestlé, was from Germany; Walter Boveri, founder of ASEA Brown Boveri (ABB) and famed for his heavy electric machinery, was also from Germany; Leo Henryk Sternbach, who saved the pharmaceutical company Roche by developing barium, was from Poland; and Nicolas G. Hayek, the founder of the world-famous watchmaker Swatch, was from Lebanon. These people, in order to make a living in a foreign country, tackled new businesses and learnt how to develop their businesses. They naturally acquired the knowledge that the markets in the neighboring countries are more promising than their domestic market.

What must not be forgotten about the Swiss history is the fact that its soldiers served actively abroad as mercenaries, or migrant soldiers so to speak. It is almost unbelievable in the present-day Switzerland, but in the olden days courageous young men went abroad because of their poor financial background at home. In those days when communication networks were not yet conveniently available, the mercenaries brought back a variety of information they acquired during their foreign services. It is said that what made Swiss banks develop ahead of banks elsewhere were contract money for mercenaries, remittances from abroad, etc. Close to Zurich, which attracts many tourists, is the town of Luzern. In this town, there is a statue of a dying lion. (Please refer to Figure 7-3.) It was constructed in memory of Swiss mercenaries who desperately defended King Louis XVI of France. It is one of the monuments that conveyed the social situation of Switzerland.

It is crucial for Switzerland to go abroad for its economic sustenance. Jean Pierre Roth, a former president of the Swiss National Bank, said that "Switzerland became successful because it was poor and small."[1]

---

[1] https://www.semanticscholar.org/paper/The-untold-story-behind-Switzerland-%E2%80%99-s-success-Breiding/0d0a3f5564be892330c6a3529d56c3139 59c9844

In recent years, the concept of a 'born global firm' has attracted attention in the study of multi-national corporations. It aims to study the firms, mostly born in Northern Europe, that are trying to develop into international enterprises right from the start. History, however, indicates that Nestlé and nearly all Swiss companies can be called 'born global firms.'

Chapter 2
Nestlé's Global Management System

1. Overview of Nestlé's Business

Let us now take a look at what kind of merchandise Nestlé is producing currently. What readily comes to mind must be the world's favorite brand 'Nescafé,' the chocolate candy 'Kit Kat,' the machine-served 'Nespresso' coffee, the world-famous ice cream brand 'Häagen-Dazs,' and the 'Frisky' cat food every pet-lover is familiar with. However, these are just the tip of an iceberg, as Nestlé owns over 1,000 brands.

Nestlé classifies its merchandise into seven broad categories. (Please refer to Figure 2-1.)

Representative products in each category are shown in Figure 2-6. Looking at the products in each category, we are surprised to find so many products that we see for the first time. We also realize that Nestlé has been expanding its business into health-related foods, pet foods and water-related areas in recent years.

What is the size of Nestlé's sales and profits? Figure 2-2 shows that the Nestlé group sales are 92.6 billion Swiss francs as of 2019, we can see how enormous Nestlé's sales of 10,000 billion yen is.

What we sell (in CHF billion)

Powdered and Liquid Beverages	Nutrition and Health Science	PetCare	Milk products and Ice cream
23.2	15.0	13.6	13.3

Prepared dishes and cooking aids	Confectionery	Water
12.2	7.9	7.4

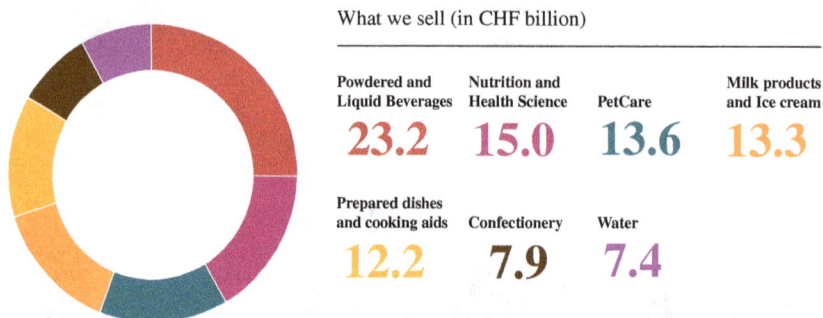

Figure 2-1   Seven Categories of Products (2019)

Source: https://www.nestle.com/investors/annual-report/facts-figures

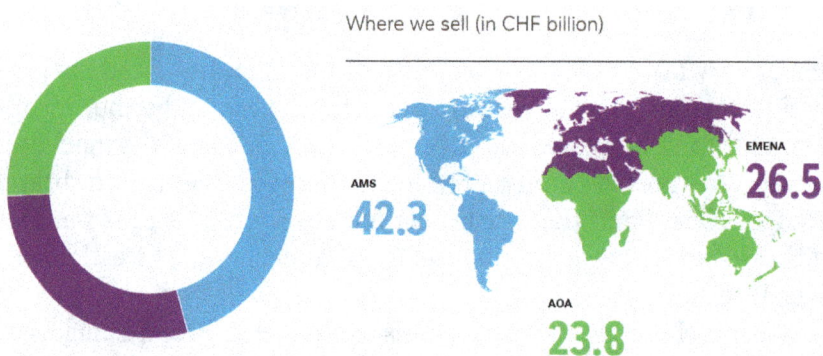

Where we sell (in CHF billion)

AMS
42.3

EMENA
26.5

AOA
23.8

Group Revenue	92.6 billion
Group Operating Profit	16.3 billion
Group Employees	291,000
Number of Countries	187
Number of Factories	413
Note: AMS — USA, Canada, Latin America, Caribbean	
AOA — Asia, Oceania, sub-Saharan Africa	
EMENA — Europe, Middle East, North Africa	

Figure 2-2   Revenue, Profit, Employees, Countries and Factories (2019)

Source: https://www.nestle.com/investors/annual-report/facts-figures

As of 2019, the total number of Nestlé employees worldwide is 291,000 with 413 factories in 85 countries, and the products are sold in 187 countries. (Please refer to Figure 2-2.) They have R&D facilities at 41 locations, including 3 science and research centers (devoted to fundamental research) and 38 product technology/R&D centers.

Although Nestlé is a European-based company, its operations in North and South America are larger than in Europe. It is growing the most in Asia and Africa, which includes China. If India is added to these areas, these are the areas that are expected to grow as emerging markets.

Looking at the numbers of employees, factories and market countries, we can see how widely and deeply the Nestlé brand has penetrated into every remote corner of the world. Nestlé is truly a super global corporation dominating the world as an 'empire of food.' Behind this dramatic business expansion lies Nestlé's M&A strategy, which is to incorporate external resources.

However, since the early 21st century, Nestlé has been altering its way of business. In 2001, then CEO Peter Brabeck declared that Nestlé would become a company devoted to 'nutrition, health and wellness.' Brabeck opined that the times had changed from the era of 'food for life sustenance' in the past to the era of 'food for enjoyment' after World War II, and then to the era of 'food for health improvement and maintenance' in the 21st century. Paul Bulcke, who took over as CEO in 2008, continued Brabeck's policy. In 2017, Nestlé tapped an outsider (whose career was not in the food business) as its CEO for the first time. Ulf Mark Schneider, who was born in Germany, had previously demonstrated a strong and successful leadership in pharmaceutical and health-care businesses.

The Nestlé Roadmap features 12 factors of operational pillars, growth drivers and competitive advantages in order to achieve 'Nutrition, Health & Wellness.' (Please refer to Figure 2-3.) As evidenced from the roadmap, Nestlé considers emerging markets as the source of its future growth and tries to develop low-price

The Nestlé Roadmap to
Good Food, Good Life

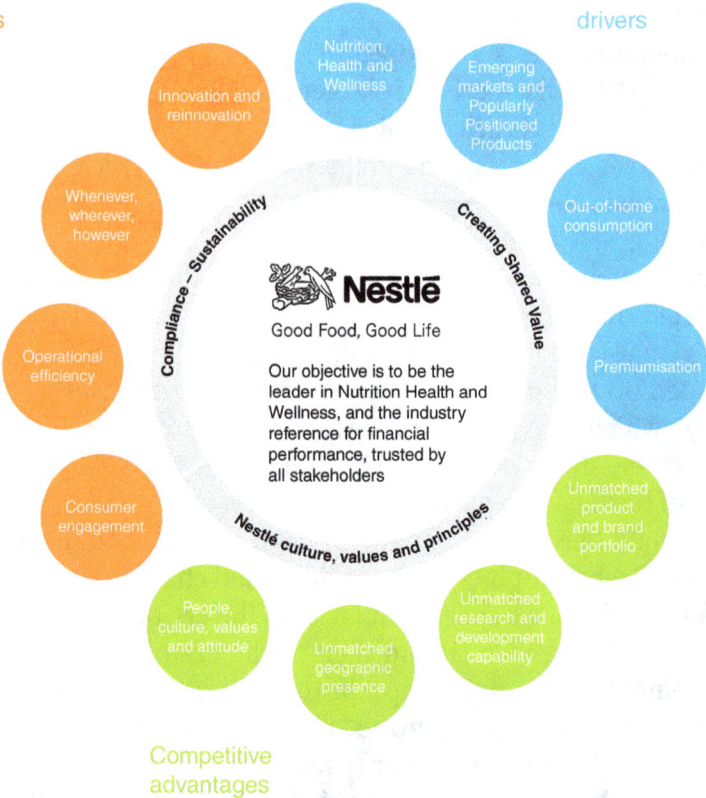

Figure 2-3   The Nestlé Roadmap

products adapted to such markets. It also tries to develop out-of-home consumption (like in offices) as seen in products such as Nespresso, by making use of its strength in global R&D, its diverse human resources and its competitive strength built up with its consumers worldwide. (Please refer to Figure 2-4 for the number of Nestlé factories worldwide and their host countries.) I have actually seen Nestlé's products adapted to the emerging markets in a showroom at the Nestlé headquarters. They are certainly low-priced and packed in consumer-friendly small packages. That is something different from other companies we see around us; that is Nestlé's distinctive finesse.

Factories

Americas (AMS)								
Argentina	6	●	●	●	●	●		●
Bolivia	1						●	
Brazil	16	●	●	●	●	●	●	●
Canada	6	●	●	●	●	●	●	●
Chile	9	●		●	●	●	●	●
Colombia	5	●		●	●	●	●	●
Cuba	3		●	●				
Dominican Republic	2	●		●		●		
Ecuador	4	●		●	●	●	●	
Guatemala	2	●		●		●		
Mexico	13	●	●	●	●	●	●	●
Nicaragua	1	●		●				
Panama	2			●		●		
Peru	1	●		●	●	●	●	
Trinidad and Tobago	1	●		●				
United States	77	●	●	●	●	●	●	●
Uruguay	2	●				●	●	
Venezuela	5	●		●	●	●	●	●

Figure 2-4 Nestlé's Factories Around the World (*Continued*)

Europe, Middle East and North Africa (EMENA)

Country								
Algeria	2	●	●	●				
Bahrain	1		●					
Belgium	1		●					
Bulgaria	1						●	
Czech Republic	3					●	●	
Denmark	1					●		
Egypt	2	●	●	●	●	●	●	
Finland	2				●	●		
France	18	●	●	●	●	●		●
Germany	13	●		●	●	●	●	●
Greece	2	●	●					
Hungary	2	●					●	●
Iran	2	●	●		●			
Iraq*	1							
Ireland	1				●			
Israel	8	●		●	●	●	●	
Italy	9		●			●	●	●
Jordan	1		●					
Lebanon	2		●					
Morocco	1	●		●				
Netherlands	1				●			
Poland	5	●	●	●	●	●	●	●
Portuganl	2	●		●	●			
Qatar	1		●					
Republic of Serbia	1	●				●	●	
Romania*	1							
Russia	6	●		●	●	●	●	●
Saudi Arabia	7		●					
Slovak Republic	1					●		
Spain	10	●	●	●	●	●	●	●
Sweden	1	●						
Switzerland	10	●	●		●	●	●	
Syria*	1							
Tunisia	1	●		●				
Turkey	3	●	●			●	●	
Ukraine	3	●					●	
United Arab Emirates	4	●	●	●		●	●	
United Kingdom	9	●	●	●			●	●
Uzbekistan	1		●	●				

Figure 2-4   (*Continued*)

Asia, Oceania and sub-Saharan Africa (AOA)

Country	No.	Powdered and Liquid Beverages	Water	Milk products and Ice cream	Nutrition and Health Science	Prepared dishes and cooking aids	Confectionery	PetCare
Angola	1			●				
Australia	7	●		●	●	●	●	●
Bangladesh	1	●			●	●		
Cameroon	1	●		●		●		
Côte d'Ivoire	2	●				●		
Ethiopia	1		●					
Ghana	1	●		●	●		●	
Greater China Region	31	●	●	●	●	●	●	●
India	7	●		●	●	●	●	
Indonesia	3	●		●	●			
Japan	3	●		●	●		●	
Kenya	1	●		●	●	●		
Malaysia	6	●		●	●	●	●	
Myanmar	1	●		●				
New Zealand	2					●	●	●
Nigeria	3	●	●		●	●	●	
Pakistan	4	●	●	●	●	●		
Papua New Guinea	1	●		●		●		
Philippines	5	●		●	●	●		
Republic of Korea	1	●	●					
Senegal	1			●		●		
Singapore	2	●		●	●			
South Africa	5	●		●	●	●	●	
Sri Lanka	1	●		●		●		
Thailand	8	●	●	●	●	●		●
Vietnam	6	●	●	●	●	●		
Zimbabwe	1	●		●	●	●		

The figure in black after the country denotes the number of factories.

*Idle factory

● Powdered and Liquid Beverages
● Water
● Milk products and Ice cream
● Nutrition and Health Science
● Prepared dishes and cooking aids
● Confectionery
● PetCare

Nestlé Annual Review 2019

Figure 2-4   *(Continued)*

2. Overview of Nestlé's Management System

(1) *Organizational Structure*

What is the management system of Nestlé, a company that has penetrated into as many countries as the number of UN member states? This subject is among the most interesting topics in the study of the development and structure of multi-national corporations.

In the case of a single-line business handling a nearly single-line merchandise, it must be easier to build a global management system adapted to each country or area. In the automobile industry, for example, there may be product groups of luxury cars, compact cars, low-priced cars, etc., but they are all classified into a single-line product of 'automobile.' For automobile companies, it is not so difficult to build their management systems specifically adapted to each market or area while carrying out their manufacturing and sales activities in various countries and areas of the world.

On the other hand, however, for a diversified company which handles multiple types of products that are operating abroad, problems arise as to whether the management system should be product-type-oriented, operation-type-oriented or geographical-area-oriented, and also who will eventually be responsible for the operation in the area. Since the aim of a business is to sustain its operations, the ultimate responsibility lies with the person in charge of the operations.

The accountability structure in multi-national corporations (MNC) is the product-type-oriented system. However, when the company's business scale in its host countries becomes bigger than that in its birth country, it becomes an important strategic issue for the management system to be situated within its market area. That is to say, the problem for an advanced MNC is how to build up its divisional management system.

One method is the establishment of the matrix management system or the regional headquarters system, covering both functional and geographical areas. It is an ideal organizational structure for MNCs, and there are some MNCs being operated in such a manner. However, there remains a number of problems in the matrix management system and the regional headquarters system in matters such as ultimate accountability, dual organization structure, etc.

What should be the management control system of corporations that have expanded to many countries and areas with diversified product divisions? How far should the corporate headquarters, which is the command center, be involved in each operation or market? The problem is how to harmonize the centralization function of the headquarters and the decentralization function of each operating division. The centralization function and decentralization function of an organization is a fundamental subject in organization theory. This issue exactly applies to corporate organizations: that is, centralization to headquarters or decentralization to each operating division is a fundamental issue in corporate strategy. "Structure follows strategy" is Alfred Chandler's famous quote. For any corporation, it is important to maintain flexibility in response to changing realities, whether in the management system or organizational structure, so as to gear towards operational diversification and expansion beyond its own country.

(2) *Business Domain*

Nestlé is a hugely diversified company handling a large variety of merchandises. Nestlé's market is global. However, Nestlé's business domain is by and large in food products, which are closely related to our daily lives. In order to make this stance firmer, Nestlé sets out its fundamental business principles as follows:

① Operate business as a food manufacturer instead of becoming a conglomerate. However, it is involved, though limitedly, in health-care business from its strategic viewpoint.

② Specialize in processed foods in its food business, but not being particular about intra-company vertical integration.

→ Stay away from upstream agri-business or raw material distribution, and also from downstream food distribution or out-of-home food service.

③ Hold global brands in the main categories of processed foods, demonstrating its sales power as a comprehensive food manufacturer to distributors.

④ Win a large market share with the brand portfolio under the Nestlé umbrella, and also by bringing influential local brands under Nestlé's control by acquisition.

⑤ Put emphasis on inter-operational and inter-regional balances in order to maintain a stable performance. Avoid too much dependence on the locality in operating each business line. Also avoid abrupt changes in business structure.

In such a way, Nestlé is aiming at expanding its ancillary businesses, while maintaining its fundamental policy of food as its core business. However, in recent years, Nestlé is expanding into the health-oriented pharmaceutical area by way of food. This can be viewed as its strategic change towards the future. The aim is to win a large market share by bringing local brands under its umbrella in addition to its own brands. While Nestlé has been aggressive in M&A in the past, it aims to be the market leader in this field also.

(3) *What is Its 'Hands-on Approach'?*

Nestlé divides its product portfolios into 7 groups and its managerial responsibilities into 3 zones. For Nestlé, which operates globally with a great variety of product portfolios, its fundamental management principle is the matrix management system, in both aspects of operations and markets at the base. Nestlé's conventional development strategy is that of external growth through M&A. The acquired companies can operate autonomously, as Nestlé is a divisional organization. This was achieved by CEO

Helmut Maucher, who was the so-called restorer of the company. He transferred management to each operational divisions as they are the closest to customers, instead of concentrating authority at the Vevey headquarters, which was previously the case.

Around the early 1990s when Maucher took office as CEO, Nestlé's performance was not good enough. Maucher believed that innovation occurs at the spot where product meets consumers, thus he gave more powers to those who are close to customers and markets, and he also reduced headquarters staff. Upon assuming office, he embarked on M&A transactions drastically. His basic principle was to minimize the headquarters' authority as much as possible and to entrust management to the acquired entities. We don't even have to worry about 'organizational theory,' as integrated management of a large variety of operations and markets by the headquarters is practically impossible. Maucher's judgment was that management should be done at the autonomous discretion of decentralized local branches.

In fact, 70 percent of Nestlé's popular items have been born in its local subsidiaries, not in its home office. This indicates the importance of locality-oriented management based on local markets and customers.

For example, the head office of Nestlé Japan is in Kobe, and it bears management responsibility for business operations in Japan. Once every three years, Nestlé executives from around the world get together at the central base in Vevey. They bring their medium-and-long term plans and give presentations there. They first have meetings with head office executives and departments, and then they give presentations in a big hall for approval. Once they get the approval, operations will be carried out on the responsibility of each local unit.

(4) *Localization of Management Responsibility*

Among the sales of Nestlé's three zones in the world, the highest is 40.7 billion Swiss francs in Zone AMS (Americas), followed by 23 billion Swiss francs in both Zone EMENA (Europe, Middle

East & North Africa) and Zone AOA (Asia, Oceania, and sub-Saharan Africa). Among the sales of Nestlé products classified by the seven categories, the highest is powdered drinks like coffee, etc., accounting for 24.4 percent of the total sales; the lowest is water, accounting for 7.5 percent.

Among them, however, there are products that are not selling well now but have future potential. The challenge is how to organize the corporate structure reflecting such developments. As seen in Figure 2-5, the managers of the three zones (Zone EMENA, Zone AOA and Zone AMS), along with the managers of water and nutrition, directly report to the Vevey headquarters' CEO. The two businesses of water and nutrition are referred to as GMB (globally

Organizational Chart

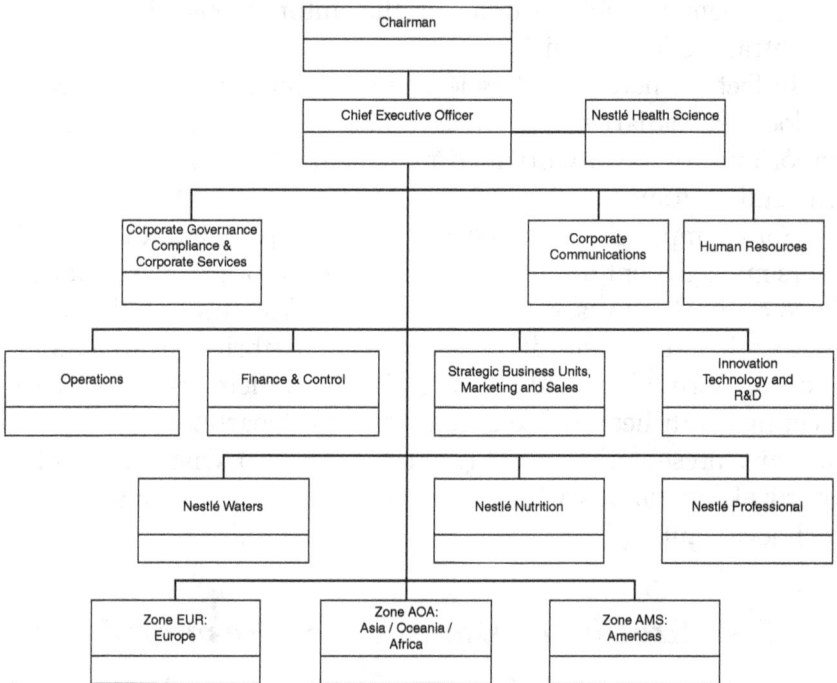

Figure 2-5   Nestlé's Corporate Organization

managed businesses), and they are in the category which should be managed globally. The three zones do not have their own headquarters but are supervised by the headquarters at Vevey. However, the zone managers are at the Vevey headquarters only during the executive meetings held once a month. Even though they have offices at the Vevey headquarters, they are moving around their territories most of the time.

Nestlé organizes the operating units, which are referred to as SBU (strategic business units), to best serve its growth. The strategic business units are grouped into six: (1) merchandise used in daily life, (2) powdered drinks such as Nescafé, (3) chocolate and confectionery, (4) ice cream and milk products, (5) precooked foods such as Maggi and (6) pet foods. Basically, those SBUs are cost centers, and profit responsibility is borne by the three zone managers.

A strategic business unit is set up for each of the main brands and marketing strategies are mapped out by in-house staff for each brand. Such staff also engage in the support and coordination of local units to carry out the strategies. SBUs are, after all, cost centers and so they do not bear profit responsibility. The basis of Nestlé's global business is its 'multinational operation system,' in which the local units operate autonomously while being given a maximum possible discretion.

Nestlé's local unit heads have the authority to determine matters concerning their business operations, such as which merchandise should be given priority in budget allocations, which merchandise should be introduced to the market and when that should be done, etc.

The local units' operation plans include the annual plan and the rolling plan for a three-year period (they annually review their medium-term plans according to changing conditions). To decide on the plans, the medium-and-long-term directions of the operations of each region are discussed among the headquarters managers in charge of each unit, staffs from the financial units and those from the strategic business units.

3. Brand Strategy

Brands of global corporations are normally classified into three categories: global brands, regional brands and local brands. Global brands are the brands known and sold practically all over the world. Regional brands are those marketed in a particular region or regions. Local brands are those marketed in one particular country. As a brand becomes regional from local and global from regional, it becomes more and more standardized. Since global brands are marketed in a wide variety of countries and areas, commonality among such areas becomes important. That relates to various factors such as consumer characteristics, legal systems, etc. Companies realize economy-of-scale benefits by operating globally while achieving standardization as much as possible. 'Economies of scale,' also called 'advantages of scale,' means the advantages obtained by reducing unit cost of production through expansion of production scale to enhance development efficiency, production efficiency, distribution efficiency, etc.

In the same way, Nestlé's brand portfolio also consists of 'world-wide strategic brands,' 'regional strategic brands' and 'local brands,' thus systematizing all its individual brands.

It is said that Nestlé owns over 1,000 brands worldwide, of which approximately 30 brands make annual sales of over 100 billion yen. Specifically speaking, 'Nescafé,' 'Maggi,' 'Buitoni, 'Milo,' 'Purina,' 'Perrier,' 'Kit Kat' and 'Contrex' are worldwide strategic brands. (Please refer to Figure 2-6.) Such brands are under the responsibility of the top management and SBUs. The SBUs prepare brand positioning strategies, labeling standards, communication criteria, packaging manuals, etc. and present them to the local units.

The regional strategic brands are under the responsibility of SBUs and the management in charge of regional markets. They are controlled with the same level of procedures as with the worldwide strategic brands, but some standards are under the approval of the regional managers.

Powdered and Liquid Beverages

NESCAFÉ | NESCAFÉ Dolce Gusto | NESPRESSO | Starbucks | BLUE BOTTLE COFFEE

CHAMELEON COLD-BREW | MILO | Nesquik | NESCAU | NESTEA

SPECIAL.T

Nutrition and Health Science

NAN | illuma | Gerber | S-26 | Nestum

Materna | Cerelac | BEBA | LACTOGEN

Nestlé HealthScience | BOOST | Meritene | ProNourish | Garden of Life

pure encapsulations

PetCare

Friskies | PRO PLAN | Beneful | ONE | DOG CHOW

Cat Chow | felix | GOURMET | Tails.com

Milk products and Ice cream

NIDO | BEAR BRAND | LC1 Probiotic | YINLU 银鹭 | Nesvita

Carnation | La Laitière | Coffee mate

ICE CREAM Nestlé | Häagen-Dazs | Dreyer's | MÖVENPICK | DRUMSTICK

Prepared dishes and cooking aids

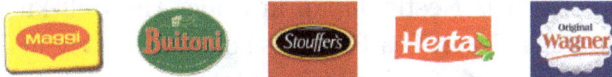

Maggi | Buitoni | Stouffer's | Herta | Original Wagner

Figure 2-6   Nestlé's Brand Categories (*Continued*)

Figure 2-6   (*Continued*)

The local brands are country-specific and are controlled by the regional units in each country. Their strategies are developed by the brand managers in each country, which are monitored by the SBUs.

Nestlé's brands that operate in more than one country total about 80 or so, hence the majority are local brands. However, it is understood that local brands do not contribute much to the consolidated sales. Usually, slow-selling brand portfolios are given up and sold off by switching to the brand portfolio under the company's own umbrella. In the case of Nestlé, however, its basic business strategy is to fit into the locality concerning all the five senses of consumers in the host countries. Therefore, decision making by the subsidiary managers is honored, and local consumers' preferences and needs are taken into consideration not only in the products themselves but also in the promotion and sales methods.

Take Kit Kat, which is very popular not only in Japan but throughout the world, for example. It comes with a variety of tastes depending on areas and seasons, and one of the global bases for its development is Nestlé Japan in Kobe. The well-known Nestlé Kit Kat Matcha Green Tea Flavor is sold exclusively in Japan and is a smash hit among foreign visitors to Japan.

4. The Vevey Headquarters (The Role of the Headquarters with 323,000 Employees Worldwide)

(1) *Three Viewpoints on the Role of the Headquarters*

Nestlé, operating a large variety of businesses worldwide, is still headquartered in Vevey, Switzerland where it was founded 150 years ago. It is literally the leader of thousands of subsidiaries all over the world, a true 'global headquarters.' Out of a total of 291,000 employees worldwide, those at the Vevey headquarters number no more than 2,000. This underscores how low the ratio of the number of the head office employees is to that of the total employees. What role is the Vevey headquarters playing? I would like to look at this question from the following three viewpoints:

First is the physical location, that is, where the headquarters should be or the issue of 'siting.' Some headquarters are sited at their places of founding. Some are moved, as they grow in their operations, to big cities that are more convenient from the managerial viewpoint. Not a few leading Japanese global corporations have their headquarters at their places of founding. Take, for example, Toyota and Panasonic, which were founded in Toyota City, Aichi Prefecture and Kadoma City, Osaka Prefecture respectively. Both of them are still headquartered in their places of founding. More than half of the Japanese companies listed in the First Section of the Tokyo Stock Exchange are headquartered in Tokyo; and many of the rest are in the Osaka or Nagoya areas. Among them are many companies not born in those areas but have moved there from their places of founding. On the other hand, many American and European global corporations are headquartered in their places of founding, and quite a few financial, service and software companies are born in big cities with their headquarters still remaining there.

The second concerns the functions of headquarters. As business expands, it is more efficient to concentrate common functions.

Such functions are finance, information system building, publicity and advertising, human resources development, crafting of long-term business plans or technology strategy, etc., as the headquarters needs to have a comprehensive view of these corporate activities. Functions that can be more efficiently carried out if handled in an integrated manner are carried out by the headquarters, so are matters that concern the group as a whole.

Thirdly, I recognize that the headquarters is where strategic functions are performed. I once had an opportunity to meet Tetsuo Suzuki, a former president of Hoya, a global corporation. He is referred to as the company's restorer. To my question of the role of the headquarters, he clearly answered, "The headquarters is the office of the top management, the CEO." That is to say, the headquarters bears a support function of devising management strategies for the top management. For that purpose, a high quality of strategy formulation with the minimum possible personnel is required.

In other words, the headquarters is the CEO's office and all that are needed are a few functions that support the CEO. In that sense, the headquarters' functions should be slim. But the smallness of the personnel does not mean fragility. Conversely, they are charged with a strong leadership role to have an overview of the company's operations. Their role is to allocate managerial resources to different priorities, taking into consideration the directions for the next step forward.

From this viewpoint, many Japanese companies are, in recent years, aiming at the holding company system. The holding company system had existed in Japan before and during World War II, but it was dissolved due to the ban on Japanese style Zaibatsu conglomerates by the GHQ (Global Headquarters). Amid increasing global competition, however, the holding company system was deregulated in 1990 out of the need for strong headquarters to unite all units of a group. Japanese food companies such as Meiji (confectionary), Suntory (beverage), Kirin (beer), Asahi (beer), etc. have a holding company system like Nestlé. The ultimate solution for a diversified company engaged in a wide variety of operations is to adopt the holding company system. Let us now examine what kind of functions Nestlé's headquarters is performing.

(2) *What is the Role of the Global Headquarters?*

Let us first consider the matter from the perspective of its physical location. I visited Nestlé's headquarters in Vevey several times. It is comprised of artistic and symbolic buildings facing Lake Geneva. (Please refer to Figure 2-7.) I still vividly remember the splendid view of Lake Geneva I had while listening to the presentation on Nestlé's management system. Anyone who has ever been there would covet working in such an environment. Vevey is close to the cosmopolitan city of Geneva. It is an ideal and convenient location, as direct flights from Geneva are available not only to major European cities but to America, Asia, China, etc., as well. It is

Figure 2-7 Nestlé's Headquarter in Vevey, Switzerland

believed that the presence of the cosmopolitan city nearby is a big factor as to why Nestlé's headquarters continues to be in Vevey.

At Nestlé's headquarters, various meetings such as top management meetings, presentations and training workshops (at Rive-Reine near the headquarters) are held throughout the year. A majority of the attendees of these meetings come from various parts of the world rather than from within Switzerland. The easily accessible location of the headquarters contributes to those events.

Those who work solely for Nestlé S.A. number only 200 or so, but there are approximately 2,000 people working at the Vevey headquarters. Most of them are employees of Nestec, which is a separate organization in the Vevey headquarters engaged in strategic tasks for the three zones, SBUs, water business, nutrition business, etc. Also included are people called the 'Mission Staff,' who are dispatched from Nestlé's subsidiaries throughout the world for a limited period of time on a project basis. They are, so to speak, intra-corporation consultants who support worldwide business activities.

(3) *The Function of the Headquarters: The Holding Company*

The formal name of Nestlé's headquarters is 'Nestlé S.A.' 'S.A.' is an abbreviation of the French term 'Société Anonyme;' it is the equivalent of 'corporation' in the United States. Nestlé's stocks are currently only listed on the SIX Swiss Exchange in Zurich, Switzerland. For a period of time in the past, they were listed on New York, London and Tokyo stock exchanges. Why are the stocks not listed on exchanges other than the SIX Swiss Exchange, in spite of the fact that Nestlé's stocks rank 13th in the world (the 1st being Microsoft, the 2nd Apple and the 3rd Amazon) with its current aggregate value of 29,700 billion yen (as of March 2019)? The reason is that due to quarterly settlements, short-term evaluations from shareholders do not match Nestlé's policy that pursues a long-term strategy.

Nestlé has achieved its growth through M&A. The shares acquired through M&A are owned by Nestlé S.A. Therefore, Nestlé S.A. is, so to speak, a holding company. The principal role of Nestlé S.A. is to make the final decision, with the minimum possible functions for such decision-making, on the distribution of managerial resources with a long-term strategy in mind. According to the Nestlé organization chart, under the Chairman of the Board of Directors is the CEO, in parallel with the heads of Nestlé Health Science and Nestlé Skin Health.

Directly reporting to the CEO are the heads of water and nutrition and the heads of the three zones. In addition, headquarters' strategic staff includes the head of the legal affairs department who oversees corporate governance, compliance, etc., and the managers in charge of organizational efficiency, corporate communication, human resources, operations, finance, business excellence, SBUs and marketing, and innovation and technology respectively. (Please refer to Figure 2-5.)

5. Corporate Governance Structure

'Corporate governance' is one of the biggest challenges Japanese companies have faced in recent years, and there has been debates and discussions about its reform. Such debates and discussions were triggered by the bursting of the bubble economy in the early 1990s which resulted in a business downturn and a wave of corporate bankruptcies. These developments raised issues such as: 'Who are responsible for these companies?' 'What is a company?' and 'For whom does a company exist?' From the Japanese point of view, a company consists of the people who work in it, and so a company exists for its employees. From the American point of view, on the other hand, a company exists through shareholders' investment, and so a company belongs to the shareholders that have invested in it, and the executive management are the representatives of shareholders entrusted with the management of the company. Therefore, if these people fail to manage the company well, their managerial responsibilities may be brought into question and they may lose their positions under shareholders' pressure. In the American way of thinking, a company is, after all, an organization that pursues economic rationality. The highest decision-making body for that purpose is the board of directors, including the audit committee and external board of directors.

In contrast, many Japanese company executives have been promoted from within, and the executives are supported by the employees as their representatives. In Japan until recently, it was comparatively rare for company executives to be called to account even if business performance had somehow deteriorated. However, in the 1990s when Japanese companies' corporate performance suddenly deteriorated due to the bursting of the bubble economy, company executives came under fire from shareholders as to who should be called to account for the business downturn. The resulting reforms brought about the separation of the board of directors and the executive board, acceptance of outside directors, establishment of the board of corporate auditors, establishment of an advisory board, appointment of female executives, etc.

Let us take a look at the corporate governance of Nestlé, a super global corporation. As seen in Table 2-1, Nestlé's board of directors consists of 15 members (as of 2019), of which 4 are from Switzerland, 3 from the United States and 1 each from Austria, Belgium, France, China and Kenya. As expected, it is a multinational lineup. Their specialized fields are quite varied, such as economics, business, law, accounting, finance, international relations, food, pharmacy, etc. The board is comprised of members who are able to challenge issues from a global viewpoint.

Nestlé's executive board consists of 12 members. They include the heads of the 3 zones and the 9 people who belong to the staff division of the headquarters. The breakdown by nationality is as follows: Switzerland 5, France 2, Germany 2, USA 2, Italy 1.

What is distinctive about Nestlé is that the Chairman of the Board of Directors and Chairman of the Executive Board are different persons. This is a German-style system, unlike those in the USA or in recent Japan. In Germany, they follow the dual board system (also

Table 2-1   Nestlé's Corporate Governance System

Board of Directors (2019): 15 Members

Chairman of Nestlé (Former CEO of Nestlé)
CEO of Nestlé
Vice Chairman, Former CEO Of Global Financial Service Firms (AXA)
Former CEO of Global Bank (Credit Suisse)
Chairman & CEO of Global Consumer Company (Inditex)
Former U.S. Secretary of Agriculture
Expertise in Asian Markets and FMCG Experience (Amway)
Former Dean of Swiss Federal Institute of Technology (EPFL)
Former CEO of Global Technology Company (Xerox)
CEO of Global Consumer Company (Adidas)
Former CEO of Global Consumer Company (Avon Products)
Former President & CEO of Global Consumer Company (Ahold Delhaize N.V.)
CEO of Global Technology Company (Harman International Industries Inc.)
Co-founder of International Business & Consulting Company
Senior Vice President of Nestlé S.A. Corporate Governance, Compliance and
   Corporate Service

Executive Board (2019): 12 Members

Chief Executive Officer
Chief Executive Officer Zone Americas (USA, Canada, Latin America, Caribbean)
Chief Executive Officer Zone AOA (Asia, Oceania, sub-Saharan Africa)
Head of Strategic Business Units, Marketing, Sales, Nespresso
Chief Executive Officer Zone EMENA (Europe, Middle East and North Africa)
Executive Vice President Chief Financial Officer
Executive Vice President Head of Operations
Executive Vice President Chief Technology Officer
Executive Vice President Global Head Human Resources & Business Service
Executive Vice President General Counsel, Corporate Governance, Compliance
Deputy Vice President Chief Executive Officer Nestlé Health Service
Deputy Vice President Head of Group Strategy and Business Development

known as a two-tier system), which consists of Aufsichtsrat (equivalent to the board of directors) and Vorstand (equivalent to the executive board). The chairpersons of the two boards are different persons. The Aufsichtsrat bears the role of deterring the head of the Vorstand and of giving advice to the direction to be taken for the future. Nestlé's Board of Directors meeting is held 10 times per year, and the average time spent per meeting is three and a half hours. The Corporate Governance Committee (a sub-committee under the Board of Directors) meets 9 times per year for an average of 4 hours per meeting. The Compensation Committee meets 5 times per year for an average of 1 hour per meeting. The Nomination Committee and Sustainability Committee meet 5 times per year for an average of 1 hour and 10 minutes per meeting. The Audit Committee meets 4 times per year for an average of 2 hours and 45 minutes per meeting.

Chapter 3

Nestlé's Basic Strategy: What is Behind the M&A?

1. Corporate Growth Method

There are two types of corporate growth methods: the 'internal growth method,' which is to gradually achieve company growth by developing internal resources; and the 'external growth method,' which is to speedily achieve company growth by acquiring external resources. The former is a traditional Japanese management style, while the latter is more of an American management style which tries to achieve dynamic growth and development through M&A.

James Christian Abegglen, who served as Representative Director of Boston Consulting Group's Japan branch, had argued as early as 1970 that Japanese companies should aggressively pursue acquisition strategy. In those days in Japan, internal growth was considered the basis of corporate management. Moreover, people had a bad impression about buying another company, as they thought that it was something like human trafficking. The first acquisition of a foreign company by a Japanese company was the M&A of Quasar's TV division in Chicago, USA by the then Matsushita Electric Industrial Co., Ltd. in 1972. Subsequent major cases include Sumitomo Rubber Industries' acquisition of UK's Dunlop Tire & Rubber (1985), Bridgestone's acquisition of Firestone of the United States (1982) and Dainippon Ink and Chemicals' acquisition of the Polychrome Corp. of the United States (1979).

M&A, which did not fit very well with Japanese companies before, is now firmly rooted in Japanese corporate management as a powerful means of managerial strategy both at home and abroad. A company's business domain would be limited if it depended on its internal resources alone for growth, and it would eventually lose out in competitions. To overcome this issue, corporate acquisition became an effective managerial strategy for furthering growth and development. However, the traditional Japanese-style management, which was based on gradually developing internal growth, had a management culture quite different from those of other countries. Therefore, not a few companies failed in the management style of seeking synergy effects through M&A. American companies traditionally considered a company as an organic economic body, and hence regarded selling or buying of the company as a natural business activity. Therefore, the M&A strategy could be said to be a traditional American way of management.

2. Globalization by Bringing in External Resources

What is the growth strategy of Nestlé, one of Europe's flagship companies? Nestlé has risen to the position of a typical global corporation through repeated mergers and acquisitions, thus acquiring external resources. Nestlé's history began when the infant milk company, founded by Henri Nestlé, merged with the Anglo-Swiss Condensed Milk Company, which was larger than Nestlé in scale. It has, thereafter, grown and expanded through M&As in the field of food business by acquiring businesses ranging from chocolate, pasta, soup, ice cream, frozen food, drinking water, pet food, health-care product to the recently-entered medicine business. Nestlé has now become a food giant.

Table 3-1 shows the major M&As Nestlé has so far engaged in. There is one management style that aims at becoming a conglomerate by tapping external growth resources regardless of the business fields. Nestlé, on the other hand, has consistently adhered to

Table 3-1 Nestlé's Major M&As

1922	Swiss chocolate brand 'Cailler'
1947	Swiss soup brand 'Alimentana'
1960	German ice cream brand 'Jopa'
1962	Swede frozen food brand 'Findus'
1968	French yogurt brand 'Chambourcy'
1973	American frozen food brand 'Stouffer'
1974	French cosmetics brand 'L'Oréal'
1976	American canned food brand 'Libby, McNeill & Libby'
1985	American canned milk brand 'Carnation'
1988	English chocolate brand 'Kit Kat' by Rowntree Mackintosh Italian pasta brand 'Buitoni-Perugina'
1992	French mineral water brand 'Perrier Group'
1998	Italian mineral water brand 'SanPellegrino Group'
2001	American pet food brand 'Ralston Purina'
2002	American ice cream brand 'Häagen-Dazs'
2006	Australian cereal food brand 'Uncle Toby's'
2007	Swiss medical brand 'Novartis Nutrition' American baby food brand 'Gerber' Swiss mineral water brand 'Sources Minérales Henniez'
2010	American frozen pizza brand 'Kraft'
2012	American medical brand 'Pfizer Nutrition'
2013	American medical food brand 'Pamlab'
2017	American coffee chain brand 'Blue Bottle'
2018	A part of American coffee chain brand 'Starbucks'

food-related businesses. However, with an eye on future trends, it has begun to engage in M&As in the health-care fields in recent years, just like a big ship gradually changing its direction. As if to steer its business to such a direction, Nestlé tapped an outsider, a German who is highly experienced in the health-care business, as its new CEO in 2016.

In Japan, during the bubble economy in the 1980s, there were many companies that tried to diversify themselves through M&As

of businesses other than those of their own. But they all failed after the collapse of the bubble economy. Since M&A is usually carried out in order to strategically utilize external resources with the company's future business in mind, the target companies are often in the same business fields as the acquirer in order to achieve a synergy effect.

Not all of Nestlé's M&As have been successful, and a number of its businesses have been sold to other companies. Unlike internal growth, M&A oftentimes brings about speedy development, but it also entails management risks and so is a difficult option to choose. Nestlé, however, has grown and developed with M&A as its basic managerial strategy. We will explore the source of its success in the following pages.

3. Business Expansion Through M&A

Although Nestlé is now a 'food giant,' for a period of 50 years from 1867 (when it was founded) to the early 1900s, it did not own such a variety of brands as it do today. Looking back at its development, that period can be considered as a run-up to its subsequent growth. Some companies last only for decades, some for half a century, and some grow for more than 100 years. The fate of a company is dependent upon whether it can change its business structure according to socio-economic changes and evolve into fresh management.

Nestlé, in response to the need for infant milk products (which were its pillar merchandise), expanded first to its neighboring countries in Europe, then to the United States, Brazil, Africa, etc. It was already known to the Japanese people as early as the Meiji Era (which was in the 1860s). The merger with its competitor, the Anglo-Swiss Condensed Milk Company, triggered Nestlé's quantum leap 40 years after its establishment. The Anglo-Swiss Condensed Milk Company, at the time of the merger, had over 20 factories with a worldwide sales network covering Africa, Asia, Latin America and Australia. This brought an ideal opportunity for Nestlé to widely distribute its products. During World War I, which began in 1914, demand for condensed milk and chocolate increased due to the need to beef up soldiers' stamina. Therefore, there was an increase in the popularity of Nestlé milk products. Initially, Nestlé was engaged in the selling and exporting of chocolates for another Swiss company. However, after reading about the prospect of business expansion, Nestlé acquired the Peter, Cailler, Kohler Swiss Chocolates Company, the company that produced 'Cailler,' the first chocolate brand in Switzerland.

Nestlé entered the chocolate business 50 years after its founding. Another 50 years later in 1988, it acquired Rowntree Mackintosh Confectionery, which was famous for its Kit Kat brand. Thus, Nestlé nurtured its chocolate brands at 50-year-long intervals into global brands.

The instant coffee Nescafé is a Nestlé original brand. It is powdered coffee, and all you have to do is just pour hot water into it. It is also convenient to carry around. Hence, it became very popular among the general public, especially as necessities for soldiers fighting in the war. Nescafé came to Japan with the US forces after World War II. In 1950, Japan started importing Nescafé in earnest. Nestlé Japan took charge of importing Nescafé, and achieved dramatic sales growth through its large-scale marketing strategy and campaign. Following the import liberalization of coffee in Japan, Nescafé began to be locally produced in Japan. The name 'Nescafé' became synonymous with 'instant coffee,' making Nestlé's presence in Japan unshakable.

Coffee beverages are now the top seller among all product portfolios of Nestlé, accounting for over 2 trillion yen. As for other product groups, sales vary; some amount to over 10 trillion yen and some less than 1 trillion yen.

Besides coffee beverages, Nestlé also expanded to other product portfolios, such as nutrition, health science products, ice cream, condiments, frozen foods, confectionery products, pet foods, and mineral water, through M&As. For example, the Maggi brand, well-known for its soups and bouillons, were acquired through a merger in 1949 with Alimentana SA, Switzerland, a manufacturer of seasonings. In the 1960s, in line with the increased demand for ice cream, Nestlé further embarked on acquiring the German manufacturer Jopa and the French manufacturer Chambourcy. Further, in 2002, Nestlé acquired the Häagen-Dazs license in the US and Canada.

4. Nestlé's M&A Strategy in the 1980s and Later

(1) *The CEO's Vision and Action*

Since the 1980s, Nestlé has grown and developed through M&As, accelerating its business expansion into pet foods, mineral water and health science.

Unlike internal growth which is gradually achieved based on internal resources, M&A requires the decision-making of acquiring an existing firm at a good timing. That is because M&A is carried out in a competitive situation. Therefore, a speedy decision-making under the CEO's strong leadership is required. A person who can achieve such a task would be an ownership-type top manager who has started up the company on his/her own, or a person considered as the company's restorer who has taken up leadership for the company's growth and development, or a professional top corporate executive that has been tapped for the position because of his/her proven ability in other businesses. Among ownership-type top executives in Japan are Akio Morita who brought dramatic development to Sony through M&A, Kan-ichiro Ishibashi of Bridgestone, Takami Takahashi of Minebea, Shigekuni Kawamura of Dainippon Ink and Chemicals (now DIC), and more recently Shigenobu Nagamori of Nidec Corporation and Masayoshi Son of SoftBank.

Selecting the target company on your own and bringing it under your umbrella through speedy decision-making is not a traditional Japanese way of management. It is an American way, that is, an external growth strategy in which you acquire external resources into your company. However, a closer look at this strategy reveals that it varies depending on the top management concerned and the business environment at the time. It is a fact that there are a number of companies developing themselves without any M&A, even among American or European companies. On the other hand, there are a number of Japanese companies that are aggressive in M&A and have achieved speedy growth. Nestlé, a European company, has engaged in aggressive M&As and developed into an unbeatable giant company in the food business.

Since the 1980s, Nestlé's CEOs have been replaced at an average of every 10 years, which means that the company has been pursuing its growth and development through a long-term M&A strategy in intervals of 10 years or so.

(2) *The Era of Helmut Maucher, the Restorer, from the 1980s Through the 1990s*

Helmut Maucher, often referred to as Nestlé's restorer, played a significant role in the dramatic development of today's Nestlé. Maucher served as Nestlé's CEO for a period of 16 years from 1981 to 1997. It is said that Maucher undertook as many as 31 M&As in 1991. Among the M&As Maucher undertook during his term of office were the acquisition of the Carnation Company known for its milk products, Rowntree Mackintosh Confectionery known for the Kit Kat chocolate, and the Perrier Group known for the French mineral water Vittel, which paved the way for Nestlé's entry into the water business.

Nestlé's acquisition of the Carnation Company amounted to 30 billion yen, which was a large-scale M&A even for Nestlé at that time. This paved the way for Nestlé's strong presence in the US market. Nestlé's share in the US market soared from 24.1 percent in 1984 to 37 percent in 1985, and its gross income increased by 35.7 percent .

The Carnation Company owned a strong brand 'Friskies' in the pet food market, a market that Nestlé was aiming at entering. The Carnation Company had 72 factories in the US and 39 factories in 17 foreign countries at that time. The acquisition of Carnation offered a perfect opportunity for Nestlé to augment its weakness in selling. Maucher recalled this event and said to the effect that it was fascinating to augment the areas where Nestlé was not strong enough. This entry into the pet food business through M&A led Nestlé to acquire an even larger pet food company Ralston Purina for 10.3 billion dollars in 2001. With this as a momentum, Nestlé's pet food business grew into a big business unit.

Kit Kat of Rowntree Mackintosh Confectionery was what one may call a representative brand and soul of the UK. Thus, at that time within the UK, there were some resistance to the M&A. But Maucher took the lead to persuade the opposition by saying that the names of 'Rowntree' and 'Kit Kat' would remain and that 'Kit Kat' would globally expand through the acquisition by Nestlé. Initially, negotiation centered around an international partnership agreement in the chocolate business with a capital investment of 25 percent. However, a competitor launched a hostile takeover bid, and Nestlé eventually entered into a friendly takeover agreement with Rowntree. Kit Kat is now being sold throughout the world and the name 'Kit Kat' is almost synonymous with chocolate. In Japan, matcha (green tea) flavored Kit Kat is very popular. Because of Nestlé's understanding that foods are fundamentally tied to local culture, Kit Kat can be adapted locally so long as the brand name and the wafer part (which is the main feature of Kit Kat) are retained. That is why we can enjoy the matcha green tea flavored Kit Kat that is exclusively sold in Japan. It now enjoys genuine popularity, particularly among foreign tourists in Japan.

Mineral water, on the other hand, is now Nestlé's almost unrivaled big business. In 1969, Nestlé acquired a 30 percent stake in Vittel, the French mineral water company. At that time, however, it was still something like a side job. But with Maucher as CEO in the 1990s, mineral water became one of Nestlé's strategic business portfolios and is now as big as its coffee portfolio. Maucher considered that high-calorie soft drinks would be shunned with the growing interest in healthy lifestyles and that the ultimate destination would be 'water.' True enough, an increasing number of people are now quite particular about the taste of water and consider water as one of their palate-pleasing drinks. Maucher also believed that the demand for mineral water would increase, as the absolute quantity of potable water still falls short of demand on a global basis. Thus, Nestlé now owns over 60 water sources throughout the world and has world-renown brands such as Perrier, Valvert, SanPellegrino, Vittel, etc. under its umbrella.

(3) *The Eras of Brabeck and Bulcke from the Latter Half of the 1990s Through to the 2010s*

Maucher, who held the CEO position for 16 years with his strong leadership, was succeeded by Peter Brabeck. Brabeck served as Nestlé's CEO for 11 years from 1997 until 2008. Nestlé's largest M&A during Brabeck's term as CEO was the acquisition of the US pet food firm, the Ralston Purina Company, for 10.3 billion dollars. Compared to the largest acquisition of 3 billion dollars during Maucher's office, we can see how big a deal the Ralston Purina M&A was. In 2002, Nestlé acquired the license of the world-famous Häagen-Dazs in the US and Canada. In 2006, it acquired Jenny Craig, Inc. (an American weight management company), and Uncle Toby's (an Australian breakfast cereal company). Further in 2007, Nestlé acquired the healthcare/nutrition business of the major Swiss pharmaceutical company Novartis for 2.5 billion dollars. In addition, it acquired the baby food business Gerber and also Swiss Mineral Water business.

Paul Bulcke succeeded Brabeck to serve as Nestlé's CEO from 2008 to 2016. Bulcke, in 2008, declared that Nestlé would transform from a food company to a nutrition/health/wellness company. This led to Nestlé's great strategy change. Bulcke continued Brabeck's long-term strategy of considering food as a means of maintenance and improvement of health in the 21st century, as opposed to food as a means of life sustenance in the past and food as a means of enjoyment after World War II.

Table 3-2   Nestlé's Major Medical Business Ventures

2007	Switzerland 'Novartis Medical Nutrition'
2010	England 'Vitaro Proteins'
2011	America 'Prometheus Laboratories' New Zealand 'Vital Foods'
2012	America 'Accera' Hong Kong 'Nutrition Science Partners'
2013	America 'Pamlab'
2015	German 'Lipid Therapeutics' America 'Seres Therapeutics' Switzerland 'AC Immune' America 'GE Healthcare'
2016	Korea 'Samsung Electronics' America 'Axcella Health'

Later on in Bulcke's term, the Nestlé Health Science Company and the Nestlé Institute of Health Sciences were established. The former is a unit that addresses the three uses of nutritional health products: medical and nursing care, general consumption and advanced therapy use. The latter is an institute where advanced research is conducted in the fields of brain health, digestion, muscle function, metabolism, etc. Table 3-2 shows Nestlé's advancement into the pharmaceutical field in recent years.

(4) *The Headhunting of Ulf Mark Schneider and Steering of a Giant Ship*

Ulf Mark Schneider, who succeeded Bulcke in 2012, was headhunted from outside the company. The German, born in 1965, did not work previously in the food business. He received a doctorate from the University of St. Gallen, Switzerland and served as a senior executive of the German multinational corporation Bayer. After receiving an MBA from Harvard Business School, Schneider joined the major German medical equipment company Fresenius as a financial executive. He served as Fresenius' CEO from 2003 to

June 2016, helping the company to become a predominant health-care business in the world. Nestlé took note of Schneider's abilities in healthcare business management and hired him. We can see from here Nestlé's shift in the direction of its long-term strategy.

5. Key Factors for Successful M&As

(1) *Strength in Information Network*

As seen so far, Nestlé has achieved growth and development through successive M&As. What is Nestlé's selection method? Usually, investment banks take part in corporate acquisitions as an intermediary. An investment bank is a type of bank that has evolved in the United States. Unlike a commercial bank that provides financial services to the general public, an investment bank is a bank that pursues profits by helping with securities transactions or as an M&A intermediary. It helps its client companies with their management strategies from the financial aspects and gives strategic advice to the companies. Being deeply involved in its client company's business, investment banks are in a position to acquire information related to corporate secrets because they engage in giving advice concerning reorganization not only of individual companies but of the industry as a whole, and concerning the synergy effect through affiliation and acquisition, etc.

Such a type of special bank as the investment bank has not existed in Japan until recently. However, institutions that play the part of an investment bank through brokering of affiliations and acquisitions between companies have started to appear in Japan. Playing such a role are Mizuho Corporate Bank, SMBC Nikko Securities Inc., The Daiwa Bank, Ltd., Nomura Securities Co., Ltd., etc. Their US counterparts are the First Boston Corporation, the City Bank, Merrill Lynch, Goldman Sachs, etc. Lehman Brothers, which went bankrupt in 2008, was also one of the leading investment banks in the US.

As for European investment banks, you might immediately recall Credit Suisse and UBS Group AG. The investment bank closely related to Nestlé is Rothschild of the UK. Rothschild, often referred to as an aristocrat of Europe, is a financial institution handling M&As among other businesses. Actually, it handled SoftBank's acquisition of Sprint Nextel Corporation in 2013, and Nikkei Inc's acquisition of UK's *Financial Times* in 2015. For Nestlé, investment banks' M&A activities are precious information sources. But the most important source is the CEO's personal network of contacts. For a CEO of the world's largest food company, it should be possible to utilize his/her personal connections on a global scale and acquire strategic M&A information on his/her own. Moreover, there are former investment bank employees acting as Nestlé's external directors.

M&A matters are handled by the financial division in the headquarters, but it is involved only in the financial analysis of the acquired companies. Thus, the ultimate judgement on M&As is made by the CEO as it is an important management strategy matter. In some cases, the financial division takes the lead, but large-scale matters are handled by the CEO himself. A variety of M&A decisions are made with a long-term view of the future in mind. Nestlé's CEOs with such responsibilities are changed at an interval of 10 years or so.

(2) *Management Principles Required after M&A*

What must be particularly emphasized in M&A transactions is post merger integration (PMI). Even though detailed investigation is conducted prior to an acquisition, a variety of managerial problems, cultural differences, etc., may arise, resulting in the failure and/or resale of the business. Nestlé cannot be an exception and has experienced a number of unsuccessful attempts because it has acquired such a large number of companies throughout the world. The number of divestments during Paul Bulcke's office in the 2010s is rather significant. Nonetheless, those businesses that have grown and developed after Nestlé's acquisition far surpass those that have been divested by Nestlé. Hence, Nestlé's M&As are largely considered to have been successful.

How does Nestlé conduct its post-acquisition management? Since Nestlé's M&As are conducted globally, it is difficult to narrow down the success factors into one. But the management method that Nestlé has always adhered to is post-M&A 'decentralization' and 'localization.' It is practically impossible for a global company that carries out an enormous variety of businesses to control everything exclusively at the headquarters. What is required is to entrust each business to the local unit to realize hands-on management catering to the local customers' needs. Johnson & Johnson (J&J), a leading US healthcare conglomerate, describes itself as an aggregate of medium and small companies. J&J has aggressively carried out M&As and grown and developed. The company says what unites the wide variety of its globally expanded businesses is its strong mission, 'Our Credo.' Nestlé also has its own mission, 'Health, Nutrition & Wellness,' and the scale of Nestlé's M&As and global businesses far exceeds that of J&J.

Inherent in the management of Nestlé, a corporation born in Switzerland, is the idea of 'cantons' that goes way back in the long history of Switzerland. Cantons are subdivided regions of Switzerland with a high degree of autonomy of their own. I wonder how many people can tell the names of the Swiss president and prime minister. Not many. It is because Switzerland is made up of cantons which are greatly independent from the central government. As administrative units that support Switzerland as a whole, cantons have strong decision-making power. Such is a matter of fact for Swiss people. Although most Switzerland-based companies are active in the international arena, what is common in them is the subdivided management system similar to that of cantons. These subdivisions as a whole contribute to the total management.

(3) *The Swiss Corporation as a National Dignity*

During the period from the late 1980s to the early 1990s when the Japanese yen appreciated because of the asset price bubble, there was active acquisition of foreign businesses by Japanese companies. With the trend as a momentum, Mitsubishi Motors Corporation tried to acquire the Rockefeller Center in New York. This attempt faced severe criticism from the American society as the Rockefeller Center was viewed by many people as an American soul.

Very recently, Chinese companies have begun to carry out M&As in Europe, America and other countries and have come under international criticism. In some countries, they met with severe opposition and had to withdraw from their attempts. M&A is basically a transaction between private companies. But when it comes to a large-scale project, it may involve matters such as national defense, technology leakage, etc., and may develop into political issues between the nations concerned. Even though it is an acquisition of a certain company, contentious political conflicts between the nations concerned may occur. It cannot be denied that there were controversial political and financial bargaining between the World War II winners and losers and also between former colony rulers and their subjects.

Switzerland has always kept a neutral stance, not leaning towards either the Western bloc or the Eastern bloc. It has never established any colonial rule, and has kept its permanently neutral policy. For that purpose, it has been necessary for the country to neutrally coexist with other countries and build conciliatory and impartial relationships with them. Among Swiss entrepreneurs in the past, there were many immigrants and refugees that had settled in Switzerland. They came to Switzerland from outside, learned the language, behaved humbly as someone from outside, and inconspicuously adapted themselves to the new environment. This experience helped Swiss companies integrate their local units abroad. It also helped them bring the acquired companies' cultures into their own. This is still true even now, and it is what has given them their competitive advantage.

The reason why Swiss companies are favored as an acquirer is that they allow much independence to the acquired. It reflects the political idea of the cantons system mentioned earlier. It is not difficult to imagine that companies to be acquired would rather choose a Swiss company as their acquirer than American, German, Japanese or Chinese companies. In considering whose umbrella to be placed under, 'national dignity' might be one of the important factors. Not only the companies to be acquired but also the general public would shy away from companies in countries where economic activities are closely connected with the political power, where corrupted business activities are prevalent or where business ethics are ignored by upstarts. The world's only country with the policy of permanent neutrality is a great soft power wielded by Swiss companies as their 'national dignity.' Nestlé's M&As, in particular, are in the fields of food, healthcare, etc. and so are not directly related to such national matters as technology export, defense, etc. Nestlé's businesses are, so to speak, in the fields of non-military peace industry. In such a sense, being under the umbrella of a Swiss company is acceptable to many people as a 'national dignity.'

Chapter 4
Nestlé's Global R&D Network

1. Perception of Research and Development

For companies, Research and Development (R&D) is the lifeline for their growth and development. They need to continually compete with each other to develop new technologies and products. So, R&D is principally conducted behind closed doors by internal staff. When we look at the history of a manufacturing company, the development of technology and product, which form the core of the company, would often lead to the founding of the company and become the locomotive for its subsequent growth and development.

It is a fact that a global corporation expands from its birth country to the global market on the basis of its domestic market. Its flagship technology and products are the source of its competitive power. Thus, R&D is principally conducted in secret within the company. However, as production becomes globalized and sales expands, it becomes necessary for corporate activities to be carried out in locations closer to the local markets.

While a product can be a real hit in its own country, the situation varies once it goes out to foreign countries, Each country has its own history and tradition, legal system, economy, culture, customs, etc. Therefore, a global company has to adapt its corporate activities to each society. Thus, R&D is also required to be localized in order to supply products suitable to each market.

We say it simply as R&D (research and development), on second thought, 'research' and 'development' are actually two different things. The former looks into the company's fundamental and exploratory issues from a long-term view, while the latter handles more practical or applicative issues from a medium- or short-term view based on the former. These two (research and development) will undergo functional differentiation in their objectives as corporate activities expand. This necessitates the establishment of a 'basic research institute' or 'central research institute' devoted to research itself and a 'development (research) institute' devoted to more practical issues, each fulfilling its particular role.

R&D can be broadly divided into those two areas as mentioned above. As the company advances to overseas markets and become globalized, not only its development function but also its research function may be established abroad. Progressive corporations, in an effort to enhance their international competitiveness, are establishing global R&D networks that link their R&D functions both at home and abroad in an organized way.

2. The Background of Nestlé's R&D Structure

Nestlé was founded by Henri Nestlé at Vevey, Switzerland and has grown into a global corporation widely regarded as a 'food giant' with a history of 150 years. A reason for its dramatic expansion is its basic policy of corporate acquisitions under the M&A strategy.

As Nestlé's core business of food is directly related to general consumers, research and development for new products and manufacturing facilities are essential. Thus, Nestlé located its research and development center close to the headquarters at its birthplace. The R&D activities at this center used to be limited to basic science research and some manufacturing technology development. However, Nestlé's merger in 1974 with Maggi, well-known for its pre-mixed soups and bouillons in Switzerland, triggered a change in the R&D structure. This merger made it necessary to integrate Maggi's R&D activities with Nestlé's for facilitation of R&D activities. Previously, all R&D activities were concentrated at the Vevey headquarters. However, since the Maggi had a large R&D facility, the R&D function remained at the acquired company. It became a good opportunity for Nestlé to form a prototype of its global R&D network. Based on this experience, it became a basic policy to carry out the R&D of the acquired company at its original location. This policy is one of Nestlé's success factors in its M&A strategy.

In 1969, a Technological Development Center was established in the Vevey headquarters. Nestlé began to place emphasis on this field, as it realized that R&D was a major factor for corporate competitiveness. Then in 1972, Nestec was established to support the entire R&D activities within the headquarters. As a wholly-owned subsidiary, it is so to speak a spin-out company that handles R&D matters. Originally handling R&D matters with several hundred employees, its role now is to support practically all aspects of corporate activities (marketing, production, engineering, employee training, etc.) in addition to its original role of research and development. The R&D unit is responsible for providing all of Nestlé's food production centers with technological support and for developing technological knowhow for the whole group.

As Nestlé's M&As increased year by year, Nestec played an active role in nurturing the R&D facilities that come with the acquired companies. At the same time, the company's expansion into the global market made it necessary to localize the R&D functions. It led to the establishment of the Technology Development Centers to enhance the development functions adapted to each locality. At the same time, Nestlé integrated the development functions of the acquired companies and strengthened its global network. Most of the centers have the term 'Research Company' at the end of their names. These centers began increasing around 1975 and totaled 16 around 1985. These facilities then increased to 21

Figure 4-1   Nestle Research Center in Lausanne, Switzerland

located in 10 countries. Seven out of these centers were directly established by Nestlé, but a majority of them were acquired through M&A.

As a result of the establishment of such a global M&A network, it became even more necessary to have basic scientific research or exploratory research into Nestlé's future development from a long-term viewpoint. Thus, Nestlé established the Nestlé Research Center (NRC) at Vevey's neighboring city of Lausanne. (Please refer to Figure 4-1.)

3. The Role of Nestec

Nestlé's R&D concerns a wide variety of businesses based on food, and its local units scatter around the world. (Please refer to Figure 4-2 and Table 4-1.) What is important is that Nestec plays a role to avoid the overlaps of the R&D activities.

As seen in Figure 2-5, Nestec is ultimately responsible for the headquarters' R&D unit and also directly related to the R&D

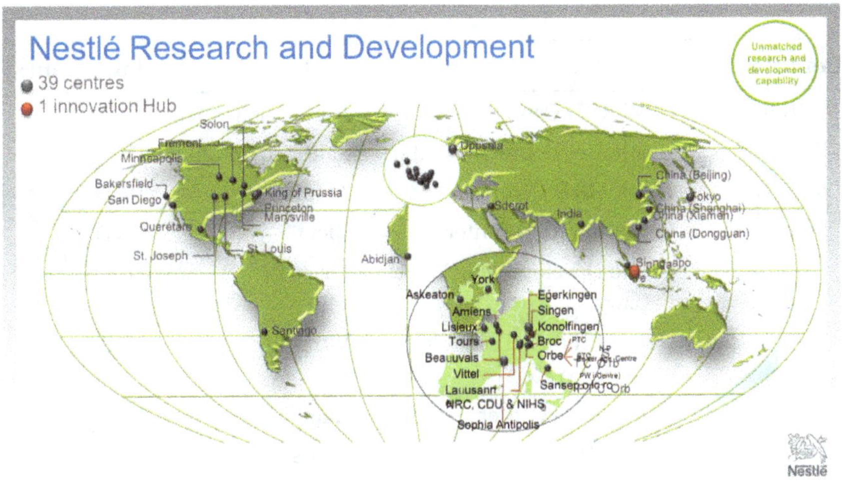

Figure 4-2 Nestlé's Research and Development Facilities

Table 4-1 Nestlé's Worldwide R&D Facilities

Country	Center Name	Location	Function(s)
Switzerland	Clinical Development Unit	Lausanne	R
	Galderma R&D Center	Egerkingen	R&D
	Nestec Ltd	Vevey	TA
	Nestlé Development Center	Broc	D
	Nestlé Institute of Health Science S.A.	Ecublens	R
	Nestlé Product Technology Center Beverage	Orbe	PTC
	Nestlé Product Technology Center Dairy	Konolfingen	PTC
	Nestlé Product Technology Center Nestle Nutrition	Konoljingen	PTC
	Nestlé Product Technology Center Nestle Professional	Orbe	PTC
	Nestlé Research Center	Lausanne	R
	Nestlé System Technology Center	Orbe	R&PTC
	CPW R&D Center	Orbe	R&D

(*Continued*)

Table 4-1 (*Continued*)

Country	Center Name	Location	Function(s)
Australia	CPW R&D Center	Rutherglen	R&D
Chile	Nestlé Development Center	Santiago de Chile	D
Côte d'Ivoire	Nestlé R&D Center	Abidjan	R&D
France	Galderma R&D center	Biot	R&D
	Nestlé Development Center Dairy	Lisieux	D
	Nestlé Product Technology Center Water	Vittel	PTC
	Nestlé R&D Center	Aubigny	R&D
	Nestlé R&D Center	Tours	R&D
	Froneri Development Center Glaces S.A.S.	Beauvais	PTC
Germany	Nestlé Product Technology Center Food	Singen	PTC
Greater China Region	Nestlé R&D Center	Beijing	R&D
	Nestlé R&D Center	Shanghai	R&D
India	Nestlé Development Center	Gurgaon	D
Italy	Nestlé R&D Center	Sansepolcro	R&D
Mexico	Nestlé R&D Center	Querétaro	R&D
Republic of Ireland	Nestlé Development Center	Askeaton	D
Singapore	Nestlé Development Center	Singapore	D
Sweden	Galderma R&D Center	Uppsala	R&D
United Kingdom	Nestlé Product Technology Center Confectionery	York	PTC
United States	Galderma R&D Center	Fort Worth (Texas)	R&D
	Nestlé Development Center	Fremont (Michigan)	D
	Nestlé Development Center	Marysville (Ohio)	D
	Nestlé Development Center	Salon (Ohio)	D
	Nestlé Product Technology Center Health Science	Bridgewater (New Jersey)	PTC

(*Continued*)

Table 4-1 (*Continued*)

Country	Center Name	Location	Function(s)
	Nestlé Product Technology Center Ice Cream	Bakersfield (California)	PTC
	Nestlé Product Technology Center PetCare	St. Louis (Missouri)	PTC
	Nestlé R&D Center	San Diego (California)	R&D
	Nestlé R&D center	St. Joseph (Missouri)	R&D

Legend
TA: Technical Assistance Centers
D: Development Centers
R: Research Centers
R&D: Research & Development Centers
PTC: Product Technical Centers

Source: Nestlé Corporate Governance Report 2019

strategy of the Nestlé group as a whole. The head of Nestec's R&D unit is also a member of the Executive Committee.

The head of the NRC and the heads of Nestlé's R&D centers throughout the world are under the umbrella of Nestec. Also, technological requirements from the global units come to Nestec and each requirement is assigned to an appropriate R&D center. Nestec has the responsibility of controlling R&D overlaps and also assigning new projects to the most appropriate centers.

Principally, Nestec staff do not engage in R&D activities themselves but are responsible for consolidating all the R&D strategies of Nestlé as a whole. Therefore, they are required to have a wide range of knowledge and ability. Personal qualities required for Nestec staff are highly skilled in human relations, substantial experience within Nestlé, maturity in age, willingness to travel on business to any place on earth, flexibility to devote themselves to the fields Nestlé is aggressively working on, etc. As Nestec R&D Center is run by a relatively small number of people, a wide range of knowledge is required rather than specialized expertise. Nestec staff keep contact with the global R&D centers and visit them at least twice a year. They also hold seminars once or twice a year with the heads and project leaders of the centers concerned.

Since Nestlé's business units spread out all over the world, these units comprise diversified human resources. Likewise, the research staff members throughout the world are diversified. There are no particular regulations about the nationalities of the Nestec staff or the top managers of the R&D Center. There is no intentional considerations to hire local people or assign someone of Swiss nationality. Aside from aptitude, human relations skills and professional abilities, there are two important criteria — language abilities and work experiences in at least two or three different countries. That is because such a person, as a leader, is required to have ample understanding of different cultures and get along well with the local researchers.

4. Nestlé's Global R&D Structure: Its Whole Picture and Framework

Nestlé, as of 2017, has 413 factories in 85 countries in the world and conducts sales activities in 189 countries. That means Nestlé products are being sold practically in all corners of the world. They also have 34 R&D bases, of which three are science and research centers devoted to research in particular and the rest of the 31 are product technology centers and R&D centers which are mainly devoted to development.

Nestlé Research Center (NRC), devoted to research in particular, is at Vevey's neighboring town of Lausanne, as mentioned earlier. More than 300 scientists and approximately 700 full-time staff members of 48 nationalities are stationed there. It is considered the world's largest private institution for nutrition studies. NRC broadly consists of the following three divisions:

- Health Science
- Material Science
- Food and Safety Analytical Science

NRC is the central base for Nestlé's worldwide R&D units and has a role of linking all the localities together. It is also involved in more than 200 scientific collaborations with outside institutions and universities, thus building a knowledge base capable of providing a quick response to changing consumer needs.

The Product Technology Center (PTC) is the R&D base responsible for putting into commercial use the ideas acquired through basic studies. The PTC is categorized according to product lines such as coffee, chocolate, seasoning, etc. It conducts studies on new technologies required for commercialization of such products: for example, the optimal shape of the capsule for instant coffee.

Nestlé has R&D centers at 27 locations throughout the world and they carry out R&D activities exclusively focusing on one individual product within the category under PTC. For example, there is a PTC for the category of instant coffee, under which is placed an R&D center focused on the study of Nescafé in particular. That is to say, each R&D center conducts basic studies on a particular Nestlé product, unlike their NRC.

In the applied development group, staff conduct studies such as modifying products to adapt to local laws, culture, tastes, etc. or conducting test-manufacture before realizing actual manufacture at each local factory. Nestlé's applied development units are located at 280 places throughout the world. In the cases of NRC, PTC and R&D centers, those at the headquarters play a leading role; but in the case of the applied development group, the local units possess a certain degree of authority. (Please refer to Table 4-2.)

Nestlé Japan does not have the PTC function, but there are applied development groups in the Himeji and Kasumigaura

Table 4-2 Nestlé's R&D Units

Basic Research Facilities	Nestlé Institute of Health Science
	Nestlé Research Center
	Nestlé Clinical Development Unit
Product Development Facilities	31 Technology Center and R&D Centers
Production Technology, Product Improvement Facilities	413 factories in 85 countries

factories. As per Nestlé's basic policy, they are allowed to modify products to match the Japanese taste and culture. Since taste often varies depending on locality, each local unit can modify a product to match the country of sale if its basic concepts are not changed. The typical example is the matcha green tea flavor Kit Kat, as already mentioned earlier. Likewise, the strawberry flavor Kit Kat also enjoys great popularity. Also, take for example the instant coffee refill packs, which is specific to Japan where environmental awareness is high. The idea was proposed by a Japanese distributor which was submitted to the PTC concerned and subsequently materialized.

The PTC advances its studies in close collaboration with the R&D Center, the results of which are developed by the local applied development group into merchandise most suited to the local needs. As such, we can see that Nestlé's R&D network is basically devoted to producing merchandise most suited to the local tastes under the authority of the local units.

5. What is 'Open Innovation'?

The idea of 'open innovation' is recently attracting attention as an issue of the global R&D network. Open Innovation can be defined as the use of not only the R&D of one's own company but also external knowledge by joining external networks in order to produce optimal technologies. Specifically, it aims to address innovation by building and maintaining open relationships with research institutes, venture businesses, etc., throughout the world who have invented and discovered new technologies. At Nestlé, approximately 5,000 people are engaged in research and development, but still it is sometimes insufficient to meet all requirements. In such cases, they collaborate with other companies beyond the boundary.

Nestlé started its Innovation Partnership Approach in 2006 and expanded its collaboration networks to universities, research institutes, venture businesses and supplier companies. For example, Nestlé launched the Nestlé Research Tokyo in June 2009 based at the University of Tokyo. It addressed a variety of health and nutrition issues such as healthy aging, metabolic syndrome, etc. In April 2016, Nestlé Research Tokyo was integrated with the newly established laboratory in Singapore.

The greatest number of Nestlé's research partners based on the idea of open innovation are located in Switzerland, but it is also in collaboration with institutions, mostly universities, in the Netherlands, Germany, the United States, Ireland, Canada, France, New Zealand, the United Kingdom, Italy, Belgium, the Philippines, China, South Korea, Estonia and Czechoslovakia.

Nestlé's open innovation network is not limited to research and development, but involves a wide variety of fields. For example, Nestlé Japan carries out businesses such as over-night delivery service of coffee capsules using ASKUL's distribution networks; behavioral data analysis of Nestlé's employees using Hitachi's technology; record keeping of conversations with customers using Softbank's human sensitivity recognizing robots; development of a system that connects a coffee machine with a smartphone in collaboration with Sony, etc. In such ways, Nestlé utilizes the idea of 'open innovation' for projects that cannot be achieved by itself alone.

6. Nestlé's R&D Center in Asia: Singapore

Nestlé's first R&D center in Asia was established in Singapore. It is the Asian unit of the NRC that is devoted to fundamental scientific research. This Asian development center was established in 1984. It is now known as Nestlé R&D Center (Pte.) Ltd., and comprises of 135 scientists and engineering/packaging/nutrition experts from 19 countries supporting product and process development. The center is located at the Biopolis, a research and development center for biomedical sciences in Singapore, under a strategic partnership with Singapore's Agency for Science, Technology and Research. Its establishment is aligned with Nestlé's long-term expansion strategy of its health and wellness business.

The world is aging rapidly due to increased life expectancy and decreased fertility rates, affecting our economic, social and medical activities. In Asia in particular, the elderly population is expected to reach 1.2 billion, which accounts for 60 percent of the total elderly population of the world. Nestlé, being aware of this situation, establishes the center in Singapore because of the high level of bio-medical research and the diverse ethnic composition in the country. Singapore is the only nation in Asia where English is an official language and is aggressive in attracting R&D institutions, universities, financial centers, regional headquarters, logistics centers, etc. from around the world. For Nestlé, the knowledge cluster in Asia is not Japan but Singapore.

Chapter 5

Nestlé's Business Ethics and CSR

1. Why 'Business Ethics' Now?

The growth of Nestlé, a 'food giant' today, has not always been smooth in its history of 150 years. The more globalized a company becomes and the stronger its brand power becomes, the more social responsibility it is expected to carry. That means the company has to take on a heavy corporate social responsibility (CSR). When a company is blessed with strong brand power, there are more chances of facing harsh social criticism once any scandal is revealed. The scandal may immediately come to light and quickly spread around the world. Telecommunication is such a convenient tool nowadays, on the other hand it can instantly broadcast corporate scandals also.

Since food companies handle products that directly affect consumers, social criticism would be severe against any act that would seem to betray consumers' trust. Material things can be replaced, but a negative image on a brand can leave a deep impression on people and cannot be easily removed. It would take considerable cost and time to regain consumers' trust. Companies that are unable to withstand such hardships would be driven out of the market and obliged to face bankruptcy. Recent scandal cases occurring among Japanese companies show how grave the social criticism can get. Typical cases of corporate scandals are bribery, window-dressing settlement, *sokaiya* corporate racketeer matters, illicit favor-giving, insider trading, tax evasion, loss compensation, automobile recalls, product liability, etc. These are all prohibited by law. Laws have coercive power, so a penalty is imposed if a law is not observed.

On the other hand, ethics lies within the heart of each person. Each person's business activities, though perfectly legitimate, vary depending on his/her ethical value. Those who ask themselves, 'Is this business activity likely to have an adverse effect on society?' would refrain from such an activity. On the other hand, there may be some people who say, 'There is nothing wrong with this business activity because it does not infringe the law.' Those who have high morality would choose the former and those who give priority to their business achievements may choose the latter. The sense of right and wrong may vary depending on the social environment one is in. Also, the sense of right and wrong may shift with the change of the times. What was not a social problem in the past may become a big social issue in the present.

An intentional illegal behavior is subjected to punishment and the morality is naturally questioned. On the other hand, people may criticize the morality of a company based on what it has been doing as its normal activities. For example, factory soot, water pollution, etc. as a result of a business-interest-first policy can be subjected to criticism. Business activities that are performed for the intention of economic growth may result in the health hazard of people and become a subject of public criticism.

2. Business Ethics as Seen from Criticism Cases Against Nestlé

(1) *Infant Formula Milk Scandal: Nestlé Boycott*

Nestlé's original goal of saving infants and benefitting society was ironically subjected to social criticism in the form of the 'Nestlé Boycott.'

During the 1960s, a number of infant food companies, including Nestlé, advanced into underdeveloped or developing countries in Africa and Southeast Asia. It dispatched its employees to maternity hospitals to provide support to child rearing in the form of formula milk. For example, newborn babies were presented with powdered milk sets. Nestlé had carried out such efforts since its founding out of the desire to save infants and also out of its global strategy of entering into the prospective growth markets. However, such efforts eventually resulted in social problems and the company was subjected to a series of accusations mostly by pediatricians and nutritionists. The reasons for the accusations were as follows:

- Formula milk made the secretion of human breast milk less active (because secretion was regulated by the baby's suckling of the nipple).
- Financially challenged families that had difficulty purchasing formula milk regularly tended to feed their children with excessively thinned formula milk, causing malnutrition among the children.
- There occurred a high incidence of infant diseases associated with the formula milk, compounded with unclean water or unsanitary conditions.

Accusations and protests started surfacing in the early 1940s, and created an international stir in the middle of the 1970s. The complaints were raised particularly by women against Nestlé, the then world-leading infant powdered milk enterprise. This led to the 'Nestlé Boycott' movement on a worldwide scale. Witnessing these developments, the World Health Organization (WHO) and the United Nations Children's Fund (UNICEF) jointly held an international meeting in 1979, and in 1981 the International Code of Marketing of Breast-milk Substitutes (WHO Code) was adopted by a majority of votes. In 1984, Nestlé fully accepted the WHO Code and the boycott issue ended. The many years of the boycott hurt

Nestlé's brand image and they were obliged to pay dearly for the recovery of public trust.

(2) *Cocoa Bean Procurement Issues: Child Labor*

As chocolate is Nestlé's major merchandise, it needs a huge supply of cocoa beans, the raw ingredient that makes chocolate. The largest cocoa producers are the Ivory Coast and Ghana. Harvesting of cocoa beans is simple and even children can do it. However, child labor under almost slave-like conditions attracted attention. Nestlé, who is the largest chocolate manufacturer and procures a huge amount of cocoa beans, could not be exempted from the responsibility. It is so to speak a supply chain management problem. The question is where and how the cocoa beans are procured and through what process the finished products are delivered to the consumers.

From the business ethics viewpoint, the higher the brand value a company has, the more serious questions are raised about the ways in which raw materials are procured. A resolution for the elimination of child labor has been adopted by the United Nations and adherence to it is closely monitored. Under such a circumstance, Nestlé set up its Child Labor Monitoring and Remediation System (CLMRS) to identify child labor cases among its supply chains, in order to find root causes and take appropriate measures. By 2015, the CLMRS has a coverage of 40 cocoa producing farmers cooperatives (50 percent of these cooperatives supply Nestlé with cocoa beans).

(3) *Water Business Ethics: Fair Trade*

Since the late 1980s, Nestlé has been emphasizing on its water business and acquiring water companies from around the world one after another. While its water business is commended as the best management strategy for the 21st century, it must be remembered that it is subject to criticism from the people who think such a business earns huge profits when a large part of the global population is facing acute water shortage. Besides, they are already receiving criticism for purchasing cocoa beans in large quantities at extremely low prices from poverty-stricken developing countries. There is also another problem of Nestlé's response to labor disputes around the world. Since Nestlé is such a gigantic company with 413 factories around the world and a sales networks covering 189 countries, there occur various problems involving business ethics in places beyond the reach of Nestlé's scrutiny. Thus, Nestlé set up its Code of Conduct and has a system to observe it. This Code of Conduct will be discussed in the following section.

3. Observance of the Code of Conduct

The idea of a 'Code of Conduct' is usually referred to as 'kigyo kodo kijun, 企業行動基準' or 'rinri koryo, 倫理綱領' in Japan. Nestlé Japan has its own term 'Nesure kodo kihan, ネスレ考働規範' which literally translates as 'think/act code.' The Japanese term 'kodo 行動' is 'behavior,' but Nestlé Japan coins its own 'think/act' term with the same pronunciation. Behind this lies Nestlé's special wish that its employees will think while they work. It clearly articulates the necessary codes to be observed by all employees. In Japan, with a series of corporate scandals since the 1990s, the Japan Business Federation (Keidanren) has established its Charter of Corporate Behavior and requested companies to observe it. Following this, similar codes have been established in most of the major Japanese enterprises.

In the United States, codes of conduct began to be established around 1970 and became prevalent in most US companies by the 1980s. On the contrary, many European companies did not have such a system and did not establish such a code until recently.

In the case of Nestlé in its history of 150 years, founder Henri Nestlé's aspirations have been well articulated in the form of its management policy but not in the form of the code of conduct. However, as its business activities in the Americas expanded, it became necessary to articulate the way toward for a new action guidelines for employees.

Thus, Nestlé established the Code of Business Conduct in 2007. (Please refer to Table 5-1.) These are translated into various languages for observance by employees.

These principles are not much different from those adopted in many Japanese companies. However, in Section 12 of its Code of

Table 5-1   Nestlé's Code of Business Conduct

Section 1.	Compliance with laws, rules and regulations • We respect the law at all times.
Section 2.	Conflict of interest • We will always act in the best interests of Nestlé.
Section 3.	Outside directorships and other outside activities • We take pride in Nestlé's reputation and consider Nestlé's best interests also in our outside engagements and activities.
Section 4.	Families and relatives • Our hiring and people development decisions will be fair and objective.
Section 5.	Corporate opportunities • We are committed to advance Nestlé's business.
Section 6.	Insider trading • We respect and follow the Insider Trading Rules when buying or selling Nestlé securities.
Section 7.	Antitrust and fair dealing • We believe in the importance of free competition.
Section 8.	Confidential information • We value and protect our confidential information and we respect the confidential information of others.
Section 9.	Fraud, protection of company assets, accounting • We insist on honesty and respect the company's assets and property.
Section 10.	Bribery and corruption • We condemn any form of bribery and corruption.
Section 11.	Gifts, meals, entertainment • We compete and do business based only on quality and competence.
Section 12.	Discrimination and harassment • We embrace diversity and respect the personal dignity of our fellow employees.

Table 5-1   (*Continued*)

Section 13.	Failure to comply • We will consult the Code, comply with the provisions and seek guidance where needed.
Section 14.	Reporting illegal or non-compliant conduct • We take responsibility for ensuring that we all act with integrity in all situations.
Appendix	Guidance on Nestlé's Commitment against Bribery and Corruption The fight against corruption/Gifts/Meals, hospitality and entertainment/Facilitate payments/Scholarships, grants, charitable contributions and non-commercial sponsorships/Political contributions/Third party compliance and Nestlé due diligence/Records and documentation

Business Conduct in particular, it is stipulated that employees must not discriminate on the basis of origin, nationality, religion, race, gender, age or sexual orientation. This global enterprise applies the code even to the board of directors and the executive board.

Concerning the ban on bribery and corruption, it is particularly emphasized in the Appendix (Guidance on Nestlé's Commitment against Bribery and Corruption). It says bribery and corruption perpetuate poverty and so Nestlé is engaged in the international fight against bribery and corruption, participating in the UN Global Compact. Bribery is an attempt to give presents, loans, rewards, etc. for the purpose of receiving favors or to receive such rewards. Such conducts are strictly prohibited at Nestlé. It also specifies that the gifts offered to third parties (such as customers, distributors, vendors, service providers, government officials, doctors, etc.) must be reasonable (in value, amount, etc.)

4. The Nestlé Corporate Business Principles

As Nestlé grows and develops through M&As, the resources for its production activities have to be procured on a long-term perspective.

Coffee beans for coffee and cocoa beans for chocolate typically need to be procured on a long-term basis. Since beans grow by adjusting to the natural environment, what will happen if they become unavailable due to changes in the global environment? Also, human activities are affected by the market economy through competition. Thus, there arises a number of problems as shown below:

- procurement of raw materials and resource development
- entry into underdeveloped areas
- environmental pollution due to industrialization
- water pollution.

In order to address these problems, efforts on a worldwide scale is required on top of the efforts by individual companies. These are not just somebody else's problems. It is important for Nestlé to address these problems in collaboration with international organizations such as the United Nations.

For Nestlé to continue growing and developing for hundreds of years to come, it is necessary to consider what should be done now. That is the challenge of 'sustainability,' which the United Nations is addressing and calling upon the world to participate. Sustainability can be defined as the ability to make the society continue for a long time in macro aspects like environment, society and economy. Above all, it is very important that business enterprises set long-term strategic goals, considering the impacts that business activities may inflict upon the environment, society and economy. Such actions have been triggered by 'the Sustainability Reporting Guidelines on Economic, Environmental, and Social Performance' and by the UN Global Compact. The details of the three performance indicators of the Sustainability Reporting Guidelines are as follows:

- Economic Performance Indicators:
  Customers; suppliers; employees; investors; public sector; others.

- Environmental Performance Indicators:
  Materials; energy; water; biodiversity; emissions, effluents and waste; suppliers; products and services; compliance; transport; overall.
- Social Performance Indicators:
  Employment; labor/management relations; health and safety; training and education; diversity and opportunity; customer health and safety; products and services; advertising; privacy; others.

The 10 Principles of the UN Global Compact are as follows:

- Human Rights
  Principle 1. Business should support and respect the protection of internationally proclaimed human rights; and
  Principles 2. Make sure that they are not complicit in human rights abuses
- Labor
  Principle 3. Business should uphold the freedom of association and the effective recognition of the right to collective bargaining;
  Principle 4. The elimination of all forms of forced and compulsory labor;
  Principle 5. The effective abolition of child labor; and
  Principle 6. The elimination of discrimination in respect of employment and occupation.
- Environment
  Principle 7. Business should support a precautionary approach to environment challenges;
  Principle 8. Undertake initiatives to promote greater environmental responsibility; and
  Principle 9. Encourage the development and diffusion of environmentally friendly technologies.
- Anti-Corruption
  Principle 10. Business should work against corruption in all its forms, including extortion and bribery.

Table 5-2   Nestlé's Corporate Business Principles

1. Consumers	Nutrition, health and wellness
	Quality assurance and product safety
	Consumer communication
2. Our People	Human rights
	Diversity and inclusion
	Safety and health at work
3. Value Chain	Responsible sourcing
	Customers and business partners
	Environmental sustainability
4. Business integrity	Ethics and integrity
	Privacy and ethical data management
5. Transparent interaction and communication	International interaction and communication
	Engagement and advocacy
6. Compliance	—

How does Nestlé respond to these guidelines? While positively incorporating the Sustainability Guidelines and the UN Global Compact, Nestlé puts the foundation of its next growth forward on creating shared value (CSV).

For Nestlé to continue advancing in response to the calls of the community, it needs to provide people with products which are of value to them. Nestlé considers this as CSV. Nestlé focuses its CSV efforts on nutrition, water resource development, agriculture and rural development. In order to realize these efforts, Nestlé set up its Corporate Business Principles in 1998. Employees are to abide by these principles and also create shared value. (Please see Table 5-2.)

5. From CSR to CSV

The concept of CSV originates from the article 'Creating Shared Value' written by Harvard Professor Michael Porter in the Harvard Business Review in 2011. Porter, a Nestlé board member then, advocated a next generation management model that would create both social value and economic value by solving social issues. CSV can be understood to be based on the further improved 'strategic CSR.' What are the differences between CSR and CSV?

(1) *What is CSR?*

The acronym 'CSR' stands for 'Corporate Social Responsibility.' CSR is currently one of the greatest challenges many Japanese companies are addressing. Each year they publish attractive CSR reports that show their efforts towards social contribution. It is said that CSR was first introduced in Japan by the Japan Association of Corporate Executives in its Corporate White Paper in 2003.

Worldwide, CSR started to come to the fore in Europe in the early 2000s as an reaction against market economy development. 'Market economy development' refers to the fall of the Berlin Wall leading to the unification of East and West Germany, the fall of the socialist regime in East-Europe, the subsequent fall of the Soviet Union, and China's transition from the socialist market economy to the free market economy. It is an effort to promote competition through liberalization of economic activities, thus creating innovation by giving incentive to enterprisers.

While transition to free market economy activated economic activities, it also brought about various social problems. Some examples are as follows: (1) disparity between the rich who achieved success in the progression toward market economies and the poor who were left behind in the competition; (2) poverty and education problems arising from such disparity; (3) reckless resource development amid economic competition; (4) global warming due to CO_2 emission through industrialization, etc. Could we afford to leave these problems as they are?

With the awareness of such crises arising in globalization and the market economy, non-governmental organizations came up with the slogan of 'anti-globalization.' Such a movement may have developed as people started to ask questions such as: what are the challenges that corporations should address, what is the essential mission of corporations, what is corporate social responsibility, etc.? CSR issues in Japan could be dated back to approximately half a century ago during the period of high economic growth, when Japan experienced factory smoke pollution problems, water pollution problems, CO_2 emission problems, etc. At that time, the negative aspects of excessive economic activities surfaced, but they were rectified. Regulations on factory sites are now tightened and so there are few cases of liability for soot pollution and water pollution.

Unlike the issues Japan experienced around the 1970s, the current CSR questions are: what is the role of a company amid the global market economy, how to view a company as part of the society, how to reconsider the primary mission of a company, etc. Corporate activities are actually conducted by each unit of the company. Therefore, it is now necessary to take a fresh look at each unit from the viewpoint of CSR. It is now required of companies to not just recognize CRS as part of their business activities, but to recognize it as their main mission and to realize what is needed to fulfill their responsibility as members of the society.

(2) *What is CSV? From Nestlé's Actual Cases*

In his essay that was mentioned earlier, Michael Porter used the term 'strategic CSR' and advocated a next-generation management model that would achieve both social value and economic value simultaneously. It is an effort to strategize the CSR within the business itself. It sets CSR at the central pillar of a business and its management strategy. This concept drew much attention as a creation of new corporate value. But it is not much different from what we recognize as CSR.

That said, what we need to consider here is that the social conditions around the 1970s when problems arose concerning CSR in Japan are quite different from what is happening now. Behind this is the rise of emerging economies. In advanced countries, CSV has taken root to some extent, if not well-entrenched. On the other hand, the BRICs (Brazil, Russia, India and China) have a chance for advancement related to CSV.

Nestlé's managerial strategy is based on such CSV. Since Nestlé is engaged in food business, setting CSV as its main issue can be a big strategic goal for them. Here I would like to introduce two typical cases related to CSV.

Coffee bean farming in the Philippines

Nestlé begun making efforts towards CSV in 2006, five years before Michael Porter introduced the idea of CSV in the Harvard Business Review. As Nestlé operates its business globally, stable procurement of raw materials is essential to the continuous running of its business. However, there is concern over the procurement of materials due to a growing population. In 1996, the demand for coffee beans in the Philippines, which is a coffee bean growing country, exceeded supply. Thus, they had to make up for the shortage by imports. The main suppliers were Indonesia and Vietnam. However, that was not expected to last long, because if Indonesia and Vietnam were flooded with coffee bean orders from all over the world due to a population rise, coffee beans would apparently run short. Worldwide shortage of coffee beans would mean a limitation in the growth of Nescafé.

The solution to this would be to increase the absolute production volume through agricultural assistance. Nestlé Philippines, from a long-term viewpoint rather than looking at short-term profits, started 17,000 cases of farmer assistance in 2010 in collaboration with the local government. They planned to raise coffee bean self-sufficiency rate to at least 75 percent by the end of 2020 from 35 percent in 2010. This plan would also bring about a side benefit to Nestlé in the long run. Farmers' income is secured through an increase in the production volume of coffee beans, resulting in the increase of middle-income households, who will in turn become Nestlé product consumers. Thus, CSV is an indispensable investment in Nestlé's long-term strategy. The CSV strategy aims at solving social problems and creating economic value at the same time through assistance to Filipino farmers.

Milk business in Moga, India

Nestlé's milk business in India started in 1962. The company wanted to enter the Indian market and it received the government's permission to build a dairy in the northern district of Moga.

Poverty in the region was severe; people were without electricity, transportation, telephone, or medical care. A farmer typically owned less than five acres of poorly irrigated and infertile soil. Many kept a single buffalo cow that produced just enough milk for their own consumption. Sixty percent of calves died newborn. Because farmers lacked refrigeration, transportation or any way to test for quality, milk could not travel far and was frequently contaminated or diluted.

Nestlé came to Moga to build a business, not to engage in CSR. But Nestlé's value chain, derived from the company's origins in Switzerland, depended on establishing local sources of milk from a large, diversified base of small farmers. Establishing that value chain in Moga required Nestlé to transform the competitive context in ways that created tremendous shared value for both the company and the region.

Nestlé built refrigerated dairies as collection points for milk in each town and sent its trucks out to the dairies to collect the milk. With the trucks went veterinarians, nutritionists, experts, agronomists and quality assurance experts. Medicines and nutritional supplements were provided for sick animals, and monthly training sessions were held for local farmers. Farmers learned that the milk quality depended on the cow's diet, which in turn depended on adequate feed crop irrigation. With financing and technical assistance from Nestlé, farmers began to dig previously unaffordable deep-bore wells. Improved irrigation not only fed cows but increased crop yields, producing surplus wheat and rice and raising the standard of living.

When Nestlé's milk factory first opened, only 180 local farmers supplied milk. Today, Nestlé buys milk from more than 75,000 farmers in the region, collecting it twice daily from more than 650 village dairies. The death rate of calves has dropped by 75 percent. Milk production has increased by 50-fold. As the quality improved, Nestlé was able to pay higher prices to farmers than those set by the government, and its steady biweekly payments enabled farmers to obtain credit. Competing dairies and milk factories began to open, and an industry cluster started to develop.

Today, Moga has a significantly higher standard of living than other regions in the vicinity. Ninety percent of the homes have electricity, and most have telephones; all villages have primary schools, and many have secondary schools. Moga has five times the number of doctors as neighboring regions. The increased purchasing power of local farmers has also greatly expanded the market for Nestlé's products, further supporting the firm's economic success.

6. Nestlé's Strategic Target Through CSV

Nestlé has set its managerial mission as CSV and is advocating it throughout the world as its strategic target. (Please refer to Figure 5-1.) In this managerial mission, emphasis is on 'nutrition,' 'rural development' and 'water' as the key areas for long-term value creation. (Please refer to Table 5-3.)

As the world's leading nutrition, health and wellness company, Nestlé has a responsibility to provide consumers with high-quality, nutritious products, regardless of where they are sold and the price

Creating Shared Value (CSV)

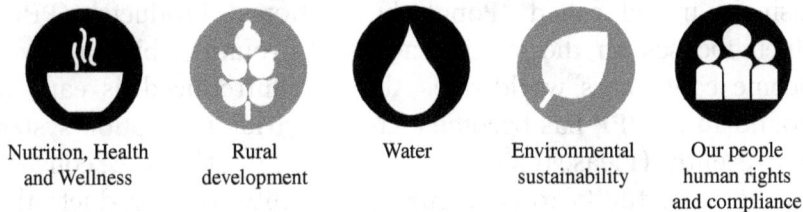

Nutrition, Health and Wellness	Rural development	Water	Environmental sustainability	Our people human rights and compliance

Figure 5-1   Nestlé's CSV Areas

Table 5-3 Nestlé's CSV Targets

Nutrition	to enable healthier and happier lives for individuals and families, with a strong focus on infants and children;
Rural Development	to help develop thriving and resilient communities, and support better livelihoods for those we live and work with; and
Water	to address an issue of critical concern for the planet and a lynchpin of food security.

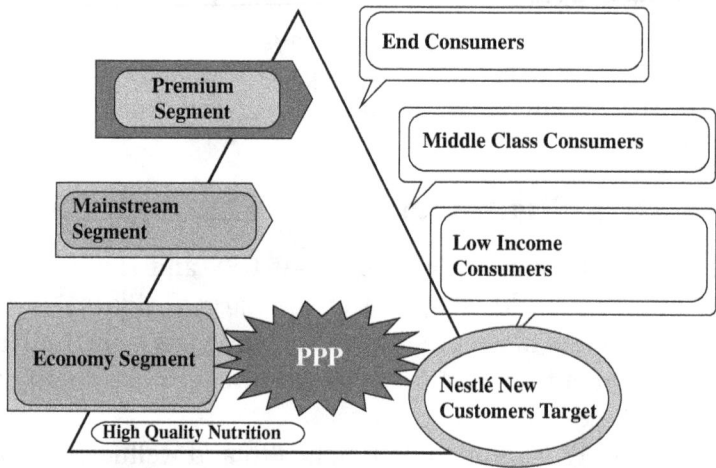

https://www.jetro.go.jp/publications/sensor/

Figure 5-2 Nestlé's PPP Strategy

point at which they are sold. Therefore, it has developed a specific business model called "Popularly Positioned Products" (PPPs) which focuses on the specific needs of around 3 billion lower-income consumers worldwide. Although introduced as early as around 1992, PPP has become a companywide promotion system only recently. (Please refer to Figure 5-2.) PPPs offer these consumers the opportunity to consume high-quality food products that provide nutritional value at an affordable cost and appropriate format. PPPs are defined as one Nestlé's main growth drivers for years to come.

Nestlé's presence in emerging markets is both highly developed, with 33 billion dollars of sales in 2009, and rich with opportunity as these markets continue to grow dynamically. Business in these markets grew faster than the rest and there is still huge potential, as the population in emerging markets is expected to increase by 3.3 billion (between 2000 to 2050). More specifically, there is an estimated one billion additional consumers entering into the cash economy within the next ten years.

Nestlé also sells PPPs in developed markets, mainly in Europe. With its diverse product and brand portfolio, it is able to cover all income levels and provide solutions to the changing purchasing patterns of the environment, adapting to consumer requirements. Its portfolio is broad based, as there are cheap and expensive versions of the same product category. Nestlé offers the possibility to trade up and trade down without trading out of its product.

The reason for 'nutrition' as a key CSV target is that food is originally Nestlé's mainstay. That familiar logo of three birds in a nest with the 'Good Food, Good Life' brand apparently underscores that its mainstay is food. As per its food strategy, emphasis is placed on providing products that contribute to consumers' healthy dietary life, giving consideration to calorie intake control and nutrient supply. However, Nestlé's products are not necessarily reaching poor people suffering from chronic undernutrition due to financial reasons or inadequacy of distribution channels. Nestlé is challenging itself to supply these people in need with opportunities for income increase in various ways. Nestlé is also challenging itself to supply nutritional supplementary foods affordable to these people, thus contributing to the improvement of malnutrition and lowering of infant mortality rate.

While Nestlé has established its global presence as a supplier of foods for average food consumers, it is necessary for it to attract new customer segments for its sustainable business growth. In emerging countries, the population of middle-income earners has increased due to rapid economic growth, and so Nestlé has been enjoying the increase of customers and sales. Worldwide, however, there still is a large population of poor people with an annual income of less than 3,000 dollars. These are referred to as BOP (Bottom of the Pyramid) with more than 3 billion poor people. Hence, Nestlé aims to reach the poor in emerging and developing countries with affordably-priced and nutritionally-enhanced products of good quality via its PPP business strategy. How to tap the BOP is a key to creating Nestlé's long-term economic value.

The examples of Philippines and India discussed in Section 5 above belongs to the 'rural development' CSV target.

As for the CSV target of 'water', Nestlé handles much of the world's water and is often nicknamed as the 'king of water.' It is said that Nestlé has water catchment sources in about 70 locations over the world. It is the world's largest mineral water supplier with annual sales (of water alone) of nearly 1,000 million yen. Well-known mineral water brands such as Vittel, Contrex, Perrier and Sanpellegrino (S.Pellegrino) are all Nestlé's products. Besides these, they market more than 50 brands in more than 100 countries in the world.

Why does Nestlé set its water business at the heart of its business strategy? That is because water is essential for our living. It is presumed that two-thirds of the world's population will be facing water shortage by 2025. The value of water is rising day by day. In the 20th century, companies like Exxon and Royal Dutch Shell built vast amount of wealth on oil. Water is often call the oil of the 21st century. Nestlé is likely to generate vast profits in this century.

7. Nestlé's Strategic Issues and Outlook

We have so far discussed CSR and CSV with Nestlé as an example. What we see is that Nestlé considers its business responsibility from a long-term perspective, giving attention to the society in the 21st century. Figure 5-3 is a matrix showing the important issues for Nestlé's management now: how it can solve, through business activities, negative side effects of the development of the global market economy. The Japanese government, in July 2018, decided

Nestlé materiality matrix (as assessed in 2018)

Importance to stakeholders

Major
- Natural resource and water stewardship
- Climate change
- Supply chain stewardship
- Over and undernutrition

Significant
- Women's empowerment
- Community relations

- Rural development and poverty alleviation
- Human rights
- Business ethics
- Responsible marketing and influence
- Product quality
- Food and nutrition security
- Resource efficiency, (food) waste and the circular economy
- Land management in the supply chain

- Food and product safety
- Changing consumer demographics and trends
- Product packaging and plastic

Moderate
- Animal welfare
- Employee safety, health and wellness
- Fair employment and equal opportunities

- Product regulation and taxation
- Geopolitical uncertainty
- Responsible use of technology
- Data privacy and cyber security

Moderate   Significant   Major

Impact on Nestlé's success

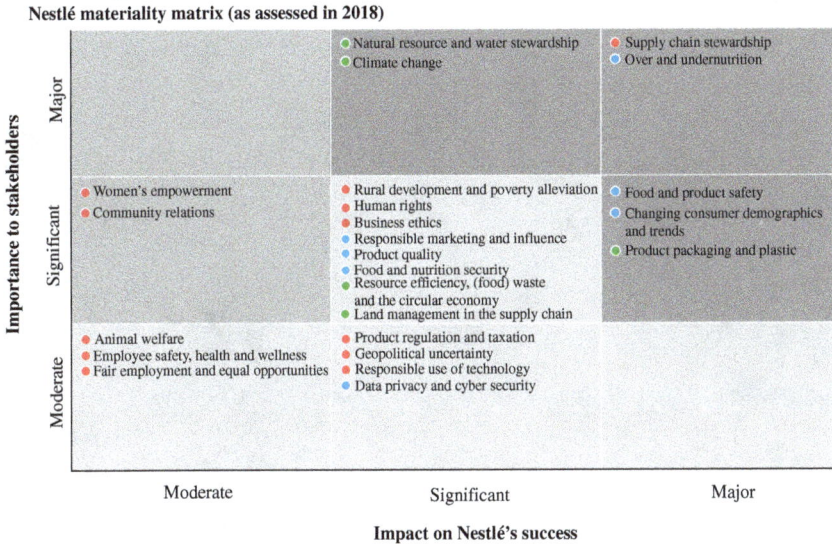

Figure 5-3   Nestlé's Major Issues Matrix

to contribute 100 billion yen to the Sustainable Development Goals (SDGs) of the United Nations. The 17 SDGs included in the 2030 Agenda for Sustainable Development were adopted at the United Nations Sustainable Development Summit in September 2015. It officially came into effect on January 1, 2016. The 17 SGDs include areas that Nestlé covers, such as food, water, local development and also education, energy, employment, infrastructure development, climate change, marine resources, ecosystem protection, etc. Nestlé is reviewing its efforts in order to promote the SDGs.

Chapter 6

Nestlé-style Human Resource Management

1. Nestlé's Human Resource Management

(1) *What is 'Human Resource Management'?*

'People,' 'things' and 'money' have commonly been cited as management resources, as well as to the recently added 'information'. Above all, 'people' is the core resource that generates new value. The phrase "The essence of management is people" says it all. No matter how much technology advances, the source of knowledge creation is always 'people.' Each member of a company plays his/her role. To consider each of them to be the most important resource is the concept of Human Resource Management (HRM).

Before the term 'human resource management' came into being, the term 'personnel management' was generally used both in the United States and Japan. It was in the 1980s that the term 'human resource management' came to be applied in the American business world. Until then, it was not uncommon for American companies to lay off their employees when their business deteriorated. Around the 1990s, however, companies began to realize that human resources are very valuable and should be regarded as the management resource that makes up the core of corporate growth.

(2) *Nestlé's Employment Style*

How does Nestlé, who has 291,000 employees, carry out its human resource management? Above everything, it is the personnel that supports the growth of Nestlé so that it can operate on a global scale. Nestlé's employees, hailing from a variety of religious and language backgrounds, are engaged in sales, production, research and development, etc. at companies directly established by Nestlé as well as at those acquired by M&A, covering not only advanced countries but also emerging and underdeveloped countries.

In such a global corporation, is it necessary to make distinction between domestic employees and non-domestic employees? Nestlé execute its human resource management without making any distinction between them in its global management system. It applies regardless of whether the company is directly established by Nestlé or is acquired by M&A.

How does Nestlé carry out its post-acquisition HRM? Nestlé's employment format is largely divided into (1) center-based employment, (2) local-based employment and (3) home-based employment. Its management format is divided into centralized management and decentralized management. Those employees under the centralized management are the center-based employees. They are the ones employed at the Nestlé headquarters in Switzerland. They can be dispatched to any part of the world. They are the ones who would spend much of their life outside Switzerland and eventually be promoted to executive positions. Those employees under decentralized management are the local-based and home-based employees. They are employed basically at the locality. While the local-based employees may work globally, the home-based employees do not.

Each unit of Nestlé recruits its personnel at its own discretion. However, employment of persons in key positions is centrally controlled by the headquarters. But not all of the key positions are held by center-based people. Some local-based employees may hold headquarters' key posts. For example, Kohzoh Takaoka, President and CEO of Nestlé Japan is a locally hired employee. Generally, the president post used to be held by a center-based person dispatched from the headquarters in Switzerland. But in Japan, the local-based Takaoka was assigned as president in 2010. While Nestlé has its established personnel policy, it is flexibly applied and even a local-based employee is assigned as top management if well qualified for the job. (Please refer to Chapter 7.)

2. Nestlé's Human Resource Policy

Since Nestlé's management resources are distributed to each business unit based on decentralized management, it is necessary to integrate them into the managerial target of Nestlé as a whole. The issue of decentralization and centralization is related to the transfer of authority. How are the leaders of such responsibility nurtured? Many Japanese advanced global enterprises, with increasing number of overseas employees, pay much attention to Nestlé's HRM.

Nestlé made HRM its basic managerial principle at the time of Helmut Maucher (the restorer). Until now, the Chief Personnel Officer, who is responsible for overseeing the HRM, is a member of the Board of Directors and the Executive Board (which are Nestlé's supreme decision-making bodies).

The Corporate Business Principles, which is so to speak a Bible to Nestlé's management, include 'Human rights in our business activities' and 'Leadership and personal responsibility.' 'Human rights' is an extremely important issue for Nestlé as it operates business throughout the world and faces a variety of labor problems not only in advanced countries, but also in advancing, emerging and underdeveloped countries, etc. Since Nestlé is the world's largest coffee company, it requires huge amounts of cocoa beans. Cocoa bean production is likely to involve child labor problems in underdeveloped areas such as Africa. Thus, careful attention must be paid. Even if Nestlé is not directly involved, it is the supply chain that is questioned, such as from where and how the beans are procured. Nestlé gives full support to the UN Global Compact and meticulously observes the rules.

Nestlé expects each member of the company to realize that the foundation of corporate prosperity is its people and to conduct himself/herself with a sense of personal responsibility. It indicates that the company recruits competent and motivated people who respect the company's values, and provides equal opportunities for their development and advancement. It also indicates that the company protects their privacy and do not tolerate any form of harassment or discrimination. Nestlé's Human Resources Policy is as follows:

- A shared responsibility:
  Line managers have the prime responsibility for building and sustaining an environment where people have a sense of personal commitment to their work and give their best to ensure the company's success.
- Joining Nestlé:
  The long-term success of the company depends on its capacity to attract, retain and develop employees able to ensure ongoing and sustainable growth.
- Employment and working conditions:
  We are committed to providing our employees all over the world with good working conditions, a safe and healthy work environment, and flexible employment possibilities.
- Total rewards:
  Attracting new hires and keeping current employment engaged is not only about remuneration and benefits based on solid performance.
- Training and learning:
  Learning is part of the company culture. Employees at all levels are systematically encouraged to consider how they upgrade their knowledge and skills.
- Talent, development and performance management:
  At Nestlé, a high performance culture supported by differentiated rewards and development is key to delivery of individual and business objectives.
- Employment relations:
  Since its founding, Nestlé has built a culture based on values of trust, mutual respect and dialogue. Nestlé management all over

the world work daily to create and maintain positive individual and collective relationships.

- A flexible and dynamic organization:
  The Human Resources management requires and supports an organization 'on the move.' Nestlé is committed to continue the journey to establishing flat and flexible structure with minimal level of management and broad spans of control.

3. How Nestlé Develops Its Human Resource

(1) *On the Job Training*

There are two main types of job training: 'OJT' ('on the job training,' receiving training whilst remaining in the workplace) and 'Off-JT' ('off the job training,' receiving training away from the place of work). The former is learning through performing and experiencing, and is tacitly accumulated within the trainee. The latter is learning through acquiring knowledge and sharing it with others.

It is often said that 'experiences rather than words' and 'workshops rather than seminars', and that trainees learn better through experience on the job rather than through theory. However, it is the theory that gives objective backing to the knowledge from experience, and hence theory is necessary for appropriate decision-making. What is important for businesses is to repeatedly engage in both types of training in parallel. By so doing, the trainees could learn to make appropriate judgements on management.

In conducting global business activities, even if meticulous analysis is made based on theory, there remain many facts that cannot be obtained except at the actual site of business. Therefore, it is important to learn through experience by associating, talking and negotiating with the people at local units abroad. The basis of Nestlé's management is the front-line principle. One's business experiences at various Nestlé units all over the world lead to the enhancement of one's ability and performance evaluation.

(2) *Off-JT: Nestlé Global Training Center*

The History of Nestlé's Training: From IMEDE to IMD

When I visited Nestlé in 1995, I dropped in at Nestlé's business school IMEDE (Institut pour L'Etude des Methodes de Direction de l'Enterprise) at Lausanne. Its predecessor was the first business school in Europe established by Nestlé and the University of Lausanne in collaboration with Harvard University in 1957. Maucher attended the IMEDE 8-month course when he became a candidate for a senior management position at Nestlé Germany. After that course was a special training for Nestlé's employees. That means he was at IMEDE for almost a full year. Maucher later reflected that IMEDE was the first international environment he had lived in. He came into contact with people from different cultures through the training course. He considered his encounter with the international environment there to be the most influential in his subsequent life.

Responding to the increasing demand for a business school in Europe, a small business school called CEI (Centre d'Etudes Industrielles) was set up within the University of Geneva, a town near Lausanne. It merged with the IMI (International Management Institute) which had been established in Geneva in 1946 (shortly after World War II) by a Canadian global enterprise Alcan. Later, in response to the requirement for a solid business school in Europe, IMI merged with IMEDE to create IMD (International Institute for Management Development). It is now one of Europe's leading business schools, along with the UK's London Business School and INSEAD in Fontainebleau, France.

Professor Dominique Turpin of French nationality was the President of the IMD from 2010 to 2016. Professor Turpin received a doctorate in economics from Sophia University in Tokyo. He also served as Visiting Professor at the Keio Graduate School of Business Administration. He is thus well versed about Japan. He resigned from the IMD president position in 2016 and is now holding the positions of the Dentsu Chaired Professor of Marketing and the

Dean of External Relations at the IMD. He still teaches at the IMD campus in Lausanne, Switzerland and also at the IMD Business School in Singapore. Businesspeople from Europe, Asia (including Japan, India and China), Africa, etc. attend the IMD. The school annually holds the Nikkei Global Management Forum in Tokyo, Japan for two days in the autumn in collaboration with Nikkei Inc. The Forum offers a good opportunity for IMD to be known by the world's businesspeople.

The Place of Encounter for Nestlé Employees: The Rive-Reine Training Center

Approximately two kilometers away from Vevey, where Nestlé's corporate headquarters is, stands the Rive-Reine International Training Center along Lake Geneva. This is Nestlé's full-fledged training center. (Please refer to Figure 6-1.) It is a historic mansion previously owned by a German aristocrat, which Nestlé bought and

2018. 08. 25

Figure 6-1   The Rive-Reine Training Center in Vevey, Switzerland

remodeled as its training center. It contains a dormitory, business school type classrooms, rooms for small groups, a cafeteria and a dining room in a dream-like environment, including a garden facing Lake Geneva. Here, Nestlé's employees from all over the world get together, brush up their job skills and interact with people from different cultures. This center, as Nestlé's biggest value sharing place, functions as 'a place for encounter.'

Besides this central training facility, training sessions are also frequently held at Nestlé's facilities in Mexico, Thailand, the UK, China, Greece, South Africa, Hungary, India, Ukraine, Romania, Turkey, Indonesia, Ghana, Egypt, Malaysia, Italy, Spain, Dubai, Sri Lanka, Zone AOA, EUR, AMS, etc. The training period lasts from three days to two weeks. The lecturers are mostly Nestlé's professionals in each field, and teachers from IMD are sometimes invited as guest lecturers. Trainees come from various parts of the world. Their airfares and accommodation fees are borne by each local unit, and the training fees are borne by the Rive-Reine Training Center.

Nestlé's employees are trained in the following areas:

- Management and Leadership
  Functional Leadership at Nestlé
  Advanced Leadership at Nestlé
  Executive Leadership at Nestlé
  Business Executive Management
  Mobilizing People to Implement Change
  Corporate Communication at Nestlé
  The Nestlé Leadership Program
  Leadership the Nestlé Way Program
- Human Resource
  Human Resource Management at Nestlé
  Leadership in Human Resource
- Marketing and Service
  Introduction to Marketing and Service
  Advanced Marketing and Sales

- Innovation, Technology, R&D
  Leadership in Innovation,
  Management in Innovation, Technology and R&D
  Leadership in Regulatory & Scientific Affairs
- Operation
  Ensuring Supply, R&D and Technology Management
  Leadership in Manufacturing and R&D
  Factory Managers
  Leadership on Procurement
  Supply Chain Management
  Globe
- Finance, Control, Legal
  Manufacturing Costing at Nestlé
  Finance & Control at Nestlé
  Costing for Decision Making and Controlling
  Financial Reporting and Governance
  Business Co-Pilot
  Enable Finance & Control to Market-it-Happen
  Legal as a Business Partner
  Leadership in Legal

4. Employee Performance Evaluation and the Human Resource Development System

(1) *What is 'Co-pilot'?*

As familiar to anyone, 'co-pilot' is a pilot who helps the main pilot in an aircraft. The prefix 'co' means 'together' or 'with;' both the captain and the co-pilot get on the plane in preparations for an emergency. One of its meanings in the *Merriam-Webster Dictionary* is defined as 'in or to the same degree.' Thus, it seems there is no sense of 'inferior' or 'superior' between the two pilots; they mutually check each other for a safe flight. Nestlé has adapted this system to its on-the-spot personnel management throughout the world.

A business consists of various administration departments and functional departments. The administration department is concerned with the company's future planning. It is generally agreed that the headquarters needs a general planning department that deals with the planning in an integrated manner. However, Nestlé does not have such a department. At Nestlé, each administration and functional department establishes its own planning. The important planning issues at such departments are 'people' and 'money.' The administration department requires investment for tomorrow's growth. The functional department requires investment on innovation with productivity in mind. Thus, Nestlé places both financial and personnel specialists in each of its business unit. For example, the role of the financial co-pilot is as follows:

- To be positively involved in strategic planning and promote it.
- To perform scenario planning accompanied by a firm backup plan.
- To give support to effective budget allocation through appropriate financial analysis.
- To give support to business performance management by providing correct information in a timely manner.
- To give support to cost management (including structural cost) with foresight.
- To make sure that the pricing strategy and margin comply with the agreed strategy.
- To promote new business initiatives.

This is the co-pilot system. Nestlé's co-pilot system is common to all its units throughout the world, and the co-pilots are well versed in the policies and systems of the headquarters in Switzerland and in the local corporations. Since each co-pilot reports the situation of his/her unit to the Financial Management Headquarters and the Human Resources Headquarters while staying at his/her unit, there is no chance of his/her taking a wrong path.

(2) *Nestlé's Personnel Evaluation and the Talent & Performance Management Solution (TPMS)*

Nestlé's human resource management system consists of four areas, which are common to all Nestlé units. (Please see Table 6-1) The first area is Performance Evaluation (PE) that evaluates the employees' annual performance. The second is Talent Assessment (TA) that assesses the employees' performance on a long-term basis. The third is Succession Planning (SP) in which one's successor is determined. The fourth is Periodical Development Goal (PDG) which plans human resource development on a mid/long-term basis.

Since personnel transfers occur within the country and internationally as well, all Nestlé's employees share a globally common system, which is the strong point of Nestlé. The succession planning system can be found in most companies, but it is mostly limited to executive levels (like department managers). In Nestlé's case, however, it is applied to all those holding management posts. What is most important for the top management is to find successors. At Nestlé, this succession planning is applied not only to the management but also to department managers and section managers. Table 6-1 shows the annual schedule for personnel evaluation and human resource management.

Table 6-1 Nestlé's Talent & Performance Management Solution

Performance Evaluation/ Year End Review/Set New Objectives (PE)	December–February — Interview by manager
Talent Assessment (TA)	May–July — Evaluation by manager
Succession Planning (SP)	May–July — Review by executive
Periodical Development Goal (PDG)	June–August — Discuss between employee & manager

5. Leader Development

(1) *Human Resource Development Planning*

Each company has its management vision and management plan. It is totally natural to base its human resource planning on a long-term outlook. Sometimes, management plan or human resource plan may not go as planned, but it is important that current problems may come to light by looking at the future. It might be impossible to perfectly foresee the future, but it is possible to envision the direction or growth of the business.

In business, unexpected situations could often occur, necessitating a drastic revision of an earlier plan. That said, if we did not make any plans, we would be unable to deal with unexpected situations. Even if we cannot perfectly predict the future, we could broadly grasp the business trend and come up with an idea which manifests our vision for the future. By so doing, we may find the strength and weakness of the company and try to fill the gap between them. Here lies the significance of 'planning.' For that, the final decision of the CEO is required. Allocation of managerial resources falls into the strategic decision-making duty of the highest level of management.

Nurturing global leaders is a popular discussion topic now. For a business to operate in the global market, which is increasingly common in the 21st century, the qualifications for a business leader is very important, and nurturing such leaders is an important issue. Many of the Japanese industries have grown mature and it is essential for them to develop their business overseas for their further expansion. In order to take part in such global business activities, not only the specialists in each field but also the leaders who can supervise them need to be cultivated. It will be necessary to determine systematically what types of leaders are required at which levels.

(2) *Career Design*

In order to produce leaders, the idea of 'career design' can be considered. It is a kind of elitist training to develop human resources while having employees experience a wide variety of jobs and work towards the most suitable post.

What is most important for companies is the cultivation of top level officers that are well qualified for doing global business. In most companies, however, they develop human resource that are well versed in their limited scope of duty in a specific area. But that is not conducive to the fostering of generalists as global leaders. It is often said that 'a good specialist is also a good generalist,' but a generalist as a leader is born by purposefully acquiring the general and broad knowledge on management through experience.

The ability to carry out one's duty as a specialist and the ability to preside over those duties as a leader to produce better results are developed at different stages. Therefore, it is very important to determine at what the stage (of a person's career) should the generalist management skills training be started. That is because the period when one can exercise one's ability to the maximum is limited both mentally and physically. If the company wants a person to exercise his/her ability to the maximum in his/her 40s or 50s, it will be necessary to develop his/her skills as a generalist while he/she is engaged in a specialist job in his/her 30s.

One of the ways to solve this problem is to consider a human resource development program which includes leader development. What a company should bear in mind here is when this program should be offered. It is extremely important for the human resource development program to offer the opportunity right when the prospective leaders can receive the training. That will also help the employees enhance their motivation to learn. Such a career design is designed to foster prospective leaders by having them experience a variety of jobs systematically and consciously.

However, if we look at the matter from a different perspective, this system may create discrimination between those given the opportunity and those who are not, resulting in morale degradation. Fear of this phenomenon must have made many companies reluctant to adopt the system. Even so, the present-day global companies need leaders, besides the CEO, to carry out their duties in various bases. It would be difficult for the present-day businesses to survive if they avoid doing important things for fear of morale degradation. Human ability is not absolute but relative. Such an ability is nurtured through person-to-person relations. Thus, it is important to systematically offer opportunities for the prospective leaders to build effective human relations.

Chapter 7

The Nation Called Switzerland: Background Behind the Birth of Multinational Companies

1. International Competitiveness: World's No. 1

Speaking of Switzerland, what comes to our mind is that the nation is a tourist spot. The beautiful towns and villages among lofty mountains and the mountain trains that link those towns and villages together offer an amazing time for tourists. The time of fresh new leaves in May through June is particularly amazing. I have visited Switzerland several times and am enchanted by that beauty. I have exceptionally fond memories of the sight as I visited Nestlé in spring toward summer.

Is this fascinating country naturally blessed with a favorable financial condition? Today, Switzerland is well-known as the host country of the World Economic Forum (the so-called Davos Convention) held in Davos, Switzerland, where politicians, businesspeople, etc., of major countries of the world get together. It is annually held in the cold winter season of January or February. Davos is close to the Italian border. It is blessed with nice sunshine even in winter. It is, therefore, a winter resort spot along with the nearby town of St. Moritz. The World Economic Forum annually publishes its 'Global Competitiveness Report,' and the 2017 version

Table 7-1   Global Competitiveness Report (2017)

Ranking (previous year)	Country
1. (1)	Switzerland
2. (2)	America
3. (3)	Singapore
4. (4)	Netherlands
5. (5)	Germany
6. (9)	Hong Kong
7. (6)	Sweden
8. (7)	England
9. (8)	Japan
10. (10)	Finland

Source: Davos Economic Forum Report

listed Switzerland as No. 1, as in the previous 10 years. (Please refer to Table 7-1.) The survey is conducted with the cooperation of the IMD, a leading business school in Europe located at Lausanne, Switzerland. I answered the survey questionnaires a number of times. It might be true that the survey results turned out to be somewhat favorable to the host country. Even so, it cannot be denied that Switzerland has maintained the highest rank for a number of years.

2. The Challenge of Switzerland, a Land of Immigrants

Switzerland is sea-less. It is surrounded by world-famous lofty mountains. Large parts of the plains among the mountains are infertile and so are not fit for farming. It is short of mineral resources. Compared with the neighboring countries of France, Germany and Italy, it can never be called a blessed country from the topographical point of view. However, since it is surrounded by high mountains, it has an abundance of snow meltwater. Thus, there is the possibly of developing the energy industry by utilizing the water resources or holding winter sports events by making use of snow and water. Even so, however, the effect on the country's economy is limited.

Jean-Pierre Roth (who served as President of the Swiss National Bank) once said to the effect that Switzerland achieved its growth because it is a small and poor country. How does this concept apply to Japan? Japan, while surrounded by the ocean, is poor in mineral resources. Japanese people have made use of the flat lands along the mountain ranges to cultivate fields. Today, Japan owes its economic prosperity to the desperate efforts of the people to survive because of its scarce resources. It therefore can be said that Japan, in a way, also achieved its economic growth because it is a poor country just like Switzerland.

Wherever you travel in Switzerland, you see large groups of tourists from all over the world. It is often difficult to distinguish between the tourists and the domestic Swiss people. As of 2019, the number of foreigners out of its total population of 8.5 million is said to be over 2 million. That is to say that nearly a quarter of the population are foreigners. Switzerland is one of the countries with highest percentage of foreigners within its total population. More than 80 percent of the foreign residents in Switzerland are immigrants from other European countries. Since it is surrounded by France, Germany and Italy, many of the immigrants are from these neighboring countries.

Immigration of foreigners into Switzerland is nothing new. Switzerland has been a nation of immigrants since a long time ago. Actually, many of the Swiss companies that are now well-known as leading global companies were founded by immigrants from abroad. (Please refer to Table 7-2.) As mentioned earlier, Henri Nestlé, founder of Nestlé, was a political refugee from Germany. To name a few others, Walter Boveri, founder of Brown, Boveri & Compagnie (BBC), was from Germany; Nicolas G. Hayek, founder of the world-renowned Swatch (a watchmaker) was of Lebanese origin; Leo Henryk Sternbach, often said to be the savior of the global company Roche which is well-known for the development of barium used for stomach examination, was a Polish Jew.

Table 7-2   Switzerland's Major Global Corporations

Corporation	Industry
Nestlé	Food
Swatch Group	Casual Watch
Omega	Luxury Watch
Richemont	Luxury Jewel
Novartis	Pharmaceutical
F. Hoffmann-La Roche	Pharmaceutical
Sulzer	Marine Engine
ABB (Asea Brown Boveri)	Transmission Line System
Givaudan	Flavors and Fragrance
Swiss Re	Insurance
Zurich	Insurance
Adecco	Human Resource Services
Schindler	Elevator

Since immigrants arrive with only the barest necessities, they generally have a strong desire to succeed in their destination country. To survive in a new country, they have to produce results and win respect in the country. Immigrants in Switzerland pay attention to foreign markets beyond the small domestic market once they realize success there. They first expand to a number of European countries surrounding Switzerland. Later on, they advance to the US, Asia, etc., and to the whole world. In doing business abroad, they have to accept the local culture and traditions and co-exist with the local people. Historically, Switzerland, unlike other European countries such as the UK, France, Portugal, etc., has not colonized other lands. This fact must have contributed to them being welcomed in the localities for their modesty.

3. The Swiss Confederation and Cantons

The Swiss official languages are French, German and Italian. Around Geneva, where international organizations are located,

Figure 7-1 Map of Switzerland

French is used. Around Zurich, which is close to Germany, German is used. Around Lugano, which is close to Italy, Italian is used. (Please refer to Figure 7-1) As clearly seen in the map, Switzerland, unlike the island country Japan, is located in the middle of a number of countries. It can be safely presumed that this topographical location has considerably influence their way of living. Switzerland has maintained an arms-neutrality policy till now and is not a member of the European Union. Furthermore, it is, though an advanced country, still not a member of the United Nations.

However, it is by no means uncooperative with other countries, and it is internationally-minded. Their internationality, in which they spare no effort in cooperating with other countries while adhering to the policy of permanent neutrality, is underscored by the fact that the headquarters and secretariats of global organizations and institutes such as the International Labor Organization (ILO), the World Health Organization (WHO), the United Nations Conference on Trade and Development (UNCTAD), the World Trade Organization (WTO) and the International Committee of the Red Cross (ICRC) are all based in Geneva.

Switzerland is no more than a little larger than Kyushu, Japan. Speaking of large cities of Switzerland, you'd name Zurich, the center of finance, commerce and industry, culture and art; Geneva, where various international organizations are located; Basel, where the Bank for International Settlements (BIS) is located: Lausanne, where the International Olympic Committee is headquartered; and Bern, the capital of Switzerland and the center of politics.

However, what immediately comes to our minds are, above all, mountains and lakes and the tourist spots among them. The leading mountains are the Monte Rosa, the Matterhorn and the Jungfrau. The leading lakes are Lake Geneva, which faces the city of Geneva; and Lake Constance, which faces the city of Zurich. Above all, though, the most alluring tourist spots are Lucerne, Interlaken, Grindelwald, Zermatt and Saint Moritz. The whole of Switzerland is high in altitude, and so it is cool in summer and cold in winter. Thus, they attract tourists from all over the world who take advantage of these seasons. The whole country is just like a national park, and wherever we go, the people's lives are simply picturesque. In order to preserve such sights, government subsidies are provided and rigid restrictions are imposed, even if it is just to build a residential house, so as not to affect the surrounding sights.

In order to get acquainted with the Swiss government system, it is necessary to understand the confederation system that consists of independent entities called 'cantons.' Presently, there are 20 cantons and 6 half cantons in Switzerland. Each of the plains surrounded by steep mountains was one unit and the people in each unit lived independently. Each unit developed its own economic infrastructure, political system, self-defense measures, etc. This led to the establishment of the current canton system. Cantons vary from big cities such as Zurich and Geneva to Bern (Swiss political center), Lucerne (a famed tourist spot) and Jura (the least populated canton).

Few of us have heard of the name of the incumbent Swiss President. Although Switzerland has a president, the president is elected at yearly intervals from among the leaders representing every canton. It is, therefore, important to understand that the whole country consists of cantons. The national flag of Switzerland displays a white cross in the center of a square red field. Each canton has its own emblem and constitutes an administrative unit. Figure 7-2 shows the emblems of the cantons.

Arms [16]	Code	Canton of	Since	Capital	Population [Note 3]
	ZH	Zürich	1351	Zürich	1,539,275[20]
	BE	Bern	1353	Bern	1,039,474[21]
	LU	Lucerne	1332	Lucerne	413,120[22]
	UR	Uri	1291[Note 5]	Altdorf	36,703[23]
	SZ	Schwyz	1291[Note 5]	Schwyz	160,480[24]
	OW	Obwalden	1291[Note 5] or 1315 (as part of Unterwalden)	Sarnen	37,930[25]
	NW	Nidwalden	1291[Note 5] (as Unterwalden)	Stans	43,087[26]
	GL	Glarus	1352	Glarus	40,590[27]
	ZG	Zug	1352	Zug	127,642[28]
	FR	Fribourg	1481	Fribourg	321,783[29]
	SO	Solothurn	1481	Solothurn	275,247[30]
	BS	Basel-Stadt	1501 (as Basel until 1833/1999)	Basel	201,469[31]
	BL	Basel-Landschaft	1501 (as Basel until 1833/1999)	Liestal	290,765[32]

Figure 7-2 The 26 Cantons of Switzerland (*Continued*)

	SH	Schaffhausen	1501	Schaffhausen	82,348[33]
	AR	Appenzell Ausserrhoden	1513 (as Appenzell until 1597/1999)	Herisau[Note 6]	55,445[34]
	AI	Appenzell Innerrhoden	1513 (as Appenzell until 1597/1999)	Appenzell	16,128[35]
	SG	St. Gallen	1803[Note 7]	St. Gallen	510,734[36]
	GR	Graubünden; Grisons	1803[Note 8]	Chur	199,021[37]
	AG	Aargau	1803[Note 9]	Aarau	685,845[38]
	TG	Thurgau	1803[Note 10]	Frauenfeld [Note11]	279,547[39]
	TI	Ticino	1803[Note 12]	Bellinzona	351,491[40]
	VD	Vaud	1803[Note 13]	Lausanne	805,098[41]
	VS	Valais	1815[Note 14]	Sion	345,525[42]
	NE	Neuchâtel	1815/1857[Note 15]	Neuchâtel	176,496[43]
	GE	Geneva	1815[Note 16]	Geneva	504,128[44]
	JU	Jura	1979[Note 17]	Delémont	73,584[45]
	CH	Swiss Confederation	1815/1848[Note 18]	(Bern)	8,606,033[46]

Figure 7-2 (*Continued*)

4. Being a Permanently Neutral Country

The term 'Permanently Neutral Country' is often used synonymously with 'pacifist nation' when referring to Switzerland. A permanently neutral country is a sovereign nation specified by the international law that such a country will not join any future wars and that other countries should respect that neutrality. However, even if the country is not provoked into war, there is no warranty that the country will never be attacked by other countries. Thus, Switzerland adopts the universal conscription system in order to protect itself from invasion. Their conscription system started in 1848 when the Swiss Armed Forces was established. All men are obliged to be examined for conscription as they reach the age of 19. All adult males between the ages of 20 and 30 are required to do 300 days of military service. Women may volunteer to join the armed forces, and there is an increasing number of women soldiers in recent years. They engage in the same service as men. Military service is compulsory for Swiss men. But if an individual declines military service for religious or moral reasons, etc., he is subjected to non-military service which is 1.5 times as long as the military service. In Switzerland, we often come across young people in military uniform with an automatic rifle in public buses or trains. They are Swiss soldiers on guard duty. Switzerland, though a small country, is a nation of armed neutrality with a strong military power. Swiss permanent neutrality is not just about a peace-loving idealism, but also a self-defense measure to protect its independence which had been learned during the long history of the multiracial nation, with a variety of languages and religions, surrounded by big countries.

Swiss neutrality was formally recognized in 1815 at the Congress of Vienna, a meeting held for the purpose of discussing the restoration of order and territorial division of Europe after the French Revolution and the Napoleonic Wars. Swiss neutrality also helped offer a place for people who fled persecution in other countries. For example, French Huguenots (a Protestant sect) fled to Geneva, across the border from France, and started watch manufacturing. It led to the development of the watch industry with the center at Geneva.

5. Swiss Mercenaries

At the heart of the capital city of Rome in Italy stands the Vatican City State, the headquarters of the Roman Catholic Church. Its total area is approximately 0.4 square kilometers (about the same as that of Tiananmen Square in Beijing). However, Vatican City is an internationally recognized sovereign country and the world's smallest independent country. It would be surprising if any tourist visiting Rome didn't visit this site. Whenever you go, there are always long lines waiting to go inside its famous buildings. In the world's smallest country stands one of the largest churches in the world, the St Peter's Basilica. On its right is the Vatican Cathedral where the Pope lives. The first people you see at the Cathedral are the Swiss mercenaries who are tasked with protecting the Pope. They are clothed in a Renaissance-style uniform. Their delicate yet gallant style is perfectly photogenic for the tourists.

Why are Swiss mercenaries performing guard duties at Vatican City? In the famous tourist town of Lucerne in Switzerland, there is a statue of a dying lion constructed in memory of Swiss mercenaries who desperately defended King Louis XVI of France. (Please refer to Figure 7-3.) In those days, Switzerland had no industry to speak of, thus many people worked as mercenaries in the

Figure 7-3   The Lion Statue in Lucerne

neighboring countries. Countries that shared borders with Switzerland, such as France, Germany and Italy, witnessed the gallant activities of Swiss mercenaries whenever there were wars and conflicts. Thus, there came more and more requests for these mercenaries from neighboring countries, resulting in mercenaries becoming an important industry for Switzerland. Nowadays Switzerland is a wealthy country, and this mercenary dispatch was something that happened hundreds of years ago.

Swiss banking, which is world famous, is said to have been developed from the handling of contract money and pensions sent by Swiss mercenaries from abroad. From political and cultural viewpoints, the mercenaries also brought back a variety of information they acquired during their foreign services, which greatly contributed to the domestic development. The mercenary dispatch is a key to learn about Swiss economic activities of the past.

Chapter 8

Learning from Nestlé: Directions for Japanese Companies

1. Laying the Foundation for Future Food Business Under a Long-term Perspective

Nestlé conducts business on a global basis, but its stocks are listed only on the Swiss Exchange in Zurich, Switzerland. For some time in the past, they were listed on the exchanges in New York, Frankfurt, Tokyo, etc., but not now. The reason is said to be that short-term evaluations from shareholders does not match Nestlé's basic policy that pursues a long-term strategy. Likewise, Japan's Suntory, also a food company, is not listed on Japanese stock markets. The long-standing whiskey manufacturer does not seem to match short-term evaluations from shareholders because brewing requires a long fermentation period. Advantages and disadvantages of listing a company in a stock market vary, depending on the company's business situation, management policy, etc. So, whether a company is listed on stock markets or not cannot be a criterion for corporate valuation. Nestlé has grown aggressively by engaging in M&As in accordance with its basic policy of taking a long-term perspective. When I visited Nestlé's headquarters at Vevey, Switzerland, I asked the AOA managers about their M&A. They all answered that the key to success is to assimilate into the locality with a long-term perspective.

It is often said that the difficulty in dealing with M&A is post-acquisition management. For that matter, Nestlé nurtures the acquired companies by respecting their corporate cultures, with a long-term perspective of 10–20 years. In order to realize this, the CEO who guides the company should stay in position for at least 10 years to take charge of its long-term strategy. In fact, Helmut Maucher, often referred to as Nestlé's restorer who aggressively adopted M&As for Nestlé's key strategic units, served as Nestlé's CEO for a period of 16 years. The subsequent CEOs also served around 10 years. Basically, all global companies share the same long-term managerial perspective for the future. However, depending on the industry, quite a number of companies find it difficult to plan long-term strategies under rapid changes in managerial circumstances.

Nestlé has food, nutrition and health as its key pillars. They all relate to food, which is one of the daily necessities of life along with clothing and housing. Besides, Nestlé commits itself to expanding into potential markets such as emerging and underdeveloped countries. Thus, its business characteristics are suitable for long-term business strategies. Nestlé's current corporate mission of creating social value is also a managerial strategy based on such business characteristics.

2. Tolerance Toward Immigrants and a Fighting Spirit

Nestlé is a company founded by Henri Nestlé, a political refugee from Germany. There are also other cases of world-leading global companies founded by immigrants as noted in Chapter 7. There are now approximately 2 million foreigners living in Switzerland out of the total population of 8.5 million, and so we can safely call it a land of immigrants. That said, most of the immigrants are from neighboring countries such as Germany, France, Italy, etc. In that sense, we could call it cross-border migrations within Europe. However, what is notable here is that Switzerland is quite tolerant in accepting such immigrants. Acceptance of immigrants is not uniformly considered by the federal government; specific policies are administered by each canton instead. Cantons try to accept immigrants for their economic vitality. There are 26 cantons in Switzerland, each of which has a strong autonomy to decide its own immigrant acceptance policy. However, different policies may be applied depending on whether the immigrants are blue-collar workers or knowledge workers.

While Switzerland is ranked the highest in the world in terms of commodity prices, wages per hour are also the world's highest. In such a country, labor-intensive manufacturing is unsuitable. They proactively accept knowledge workers who have experience in knowledge-intensive companies and international organizations. Switzerland is inherently a small country with little natural resources and limited farmland. That is why it accepts immigrants from abroad and builds its economic vitality by giving the maximum autonomy to immigrants. It has differentiated itself through immigrants from various foreign countries and has made the best use of them to develop itself.

Japan has recently started to accept foreign workers in order to supplement the shortage of local workers. In addition to this, it should consider attracting more knowledge worker immigrants. The United States has traditionally been a nation of immigrants, and a variety of innovations is still occurring today. That is because of the diversity of knowledge creation that continues there. Since Japan is different from the US and Switzerland in terms of its historical background, topographical location, etc., it is not appropriate to equate Japan to them, but we should positively pursue knowledge creation in a heterogeneous environment.

3. Strategic Successor Development

Many Japanese companies are trying hard to develop global human resources. Universities, on the other hand, are reorganizing their structures by using the word 'international' in their university or faculty names. The Ministry of Education, Culture, Sports, Science and Technology (MEXT) has chosen a number of universities as 'super global universities' and supports their projects.

I am now teaching at two of these super global universities. The particular impression I get there is that there are a lot of students who want to work abroad and in international organizations, although many young Japanese adults shy away from going abroad. There are also other students in other universities who are oriented to work abroad. Students who are born and raised in a foreign country because of their parents' work location, etc. are particularly interested to work abroad. That is because they have experienced firsthand how it is like to be living overseas. They have also naturally acquired a tacit knowledge of the world beyond Japan's shores. Much hope is being pinned on such students to serve as human resources for Japan's further globalization.

Nestlé considers human resource development the core of its strategy. For the main departments of Nestlé Japan, successors are already named, who are called co-pilots that work with the pilots in pairs like on a plane. The co-pilot is ready to be the captain just in case of emergencies. Nestlé adopts such a system. Nestlé has a training center near its headquarters in Switzerland, where Nestlé's employees get together from all over the world. The training programs are many and varied. Professional skills cannot be expected to develop in a short period of training, but 'getting together' is of great significance, and the place is referred to as 'a place for encounter.' Thus, the training target is to share Nestlé's common mission.

Nestlé, operating in 189 countries all over the world, broadly divides the global leaders of its subsidiaries and related companies into two categories, as noted earlier. The center-based employees who are willing to work anywhere in the world, and the local-based employees who are employed basically at the locality. The center-based employees consist of those who are employed for that purpose from the beginning and those who are promoted to the position. In any case, their mission is to play an active role in the global arena. Behind this is the fact that Switzerland is blessed with strong support systems for people who work abroad. Among the support systems are their proud international schools with dormitories around Lausanne and Geneva. Thanks to these, parents can work anywhere abroad without worrying about their children. Japan's global companies are now pressed to strategically develop such global human resources.

4. Clarification of Corporate Mission and Information Disclosure

It is probably quite difficult even for Nestlé's employees to visualize the entire scale of Nestlé in detail. Since Nestlé conducts business in as many as 189 countries with thousands of brands, just remembering all those names is simply a big job. Nestlé's employees all over the world stand at 291,000, and they are multinational. It is next to impossible to know exactly who is working where and how.

What is the thing that aligns the whole of Nestlé towards one direction? Although Nestlé's management is based on the front-line principle and the authority is given to each locality, managerial development as a global enterprise cannot be expected unless the aspect of centralization that leads the company towards one direction is clearly defined. For the growth and development of a global company, both centralization and decentralization are required. The company's management philosophy and founding principle serve as a mental support for the employees. Just as Nestlé's logo shows a lovely mother feeding her infants, Nestlé has developed itself in health-related businesses based on the spirit of love. The idea comes from the condensed milk which Henri Nestlé developed to save poor infants' lives. Nestlé's definite business area that ties the company together is 'nutrition, health & wellness.' Since the early 2000s, Nestlé places an emphasis on striking a good balance between social value and economic value, which is its 'CSV (creating social value) management.' The problem is how to make this known to every corner of the company. The front-line personnel who take on this task are the global leaders called 'center-based employees.'

What I have learned while studying about Nestlé is that information disclosure takes place in a variety of managerial situations. With the exception of not offering stocks at any stock exchanges other than the SIX Swiss Exchange in Zurich, Switzerland, it implements a thoroughly open network management system. Information is almost completely disclosed in all managerial aspects from corporate governance structure to management compensations, committee systems, introduction of board members, etc. This managerial attitude represents the company's strong determination in sincerely accepting criticisms from outside in order to make use of them for its future strategies. This managerial attitude can be summarized as: instead of pursuing its own management style only, the company also tries to aggressively introduce from outside whatever that contributes to its growth and development.

This attitude is manifested in the aggressive promotion of M&A strategies and global R&D strategies. As for research and development, Nestlé collaborates with external research institutions and universities around the world in addition to its own R&D networks. For its mission to be thoroughly informed, it is important for key personnel to spread and practice it and also to disclose information through documents. The 'internal and external integration' strategy does not just mean the domestic and international integration but it is a strategy that aims to strengthen the corporate mission by exposing it to the outside world through 'information disclosure.'

5. The Dignity of the Nation and Corporate Global Expansion

The greatest mission of the government of a country is to make the people happy; that is, to develop the economy and distribute wealth to the people. In that sense, politics is inextricably linked with economy. Thus, 'political economy' is the basis of a good government. A nation's prosperity is the result of the collective contribution of each economic activity. In the case of Switzerland, the domestic economy is not large enough. Thus, in order to overcome the restriction, the country has advanced to the outside world for growth and development. In that sense, Nestlé is really a typical case. In terms of both sales and profits, the international markets far surpass the domestic market.

Expanding operations overseas involves cross-border transactions between more than one nation, whatever form they may take. Overseas acquisition, in particular, is to acquire a company that has been operating in the country in question. Therefore, in some cases, there may occur some sensitive issues between nations. Sometimes, overseas advancement is stemmed in view of state secrets. Sometimes, the deal is cancelled due to opposing pressure on the side of the acquired. As noted earlier, during Japan's economic bubble in the period of the early 1990s, a Japanese real estate company tried to acquire the Rockefeller Center in New York. The attempt faced severe criticism from the American society over the purchase of what is seen as an American soul. Also, in the 1970s, Japanese companies' aggressive entry into other Asian countries met with strong opposition. Although these were individual companies' attempts in overseas expansion, we learned a bitter lesson to the effect that it required a firm policy and dignified behavior in advancing into outside markets.

Companies are judged abroad as a company of such-and-such country. The company and its behavior represent the dignity of the country it belongs to. Switzerland has grown and developed as a permanently neutral country, belonging neither to the West nor the East. And host countries accept Swiss people as those born in the host countries. How a global company contributes to the host country through its economic activities tends to be severely tested these days. That, in turn, means the dignity of the company's native country is severely tested. In this sense, many Japanese companies have won trust from various countries through their global experiences.

Switzerland, though a small country, now ranks highest in national competitiveness through its activities abroad. And what's more, it is one of the nations of dignity that fascinates millions of tourists from abroad. What is expected of Japan now is to create Japan as a nation of dignity through its economic activities. This is what is meant by 'the ethical nation initiative' proposed by Ryuzaburo Kaku, former president of Canon.

Appendix

Characteristics of Service Industry & Japanese Service Industries in Asia

1. Shift to Service Industries

(1) *Primary, Secondary, and Tertiary Sector Classifications*

What type of industry is the service sector, which is referred to as a non-manufacturing sector? Economic activity is normally classified into three categories: the primary sector, the secondary sector, and the tertiary sector. These categories are based on a classification proposed by the Australian economist Colin Clark (1905–1989). Specifically, the classifications are as follows:

1. Primary sector (First Category Industry): Agriculture, forestry, fishing;
2. Secondary sector (Second Category Industry): Manufacturing, construction, mining;
3. Tertiary sector (Third Category Industry): Electricity, gas, heating, water, transport, communication, wholesale, retail, food services, financial services, insurance, real estate, service industries, government affairs.

The primary sector is involved in the collection of resources found in nature. The secondary sector is involved in processing the collected resources. The tertiary sector is involved in providing services other than the aforementioned activities. As can be seen from the classifications above, the tertiary sector is made up of a wide range of industries.

First, let us review the change of employment ratio in Japan. Shortly after World War II, ratio of employment in 1950's primary sector was 48.3%, secondary sector: 21.7%, tertiary sector: 30.0%; 1970's: 19.3%, 33.9%, 46.8% in each sector; 2000's, tertiary up to 65.8%. The most recent ratio in 2016, primary: 3.5%, secondary: 24.1%, tertiary: 72.3%. Above all, most Japanese people in 2016 were employed in the tertiary sector (Table A-1).

Second, let us review the change of GDP ratio in Japan. In 2005, primary sector: 1.1%, secondary: 21.5%, tertiary 77.4%. The most current GDP ratio in 2016, primary sector: 1.1%, secondary: 21.0%, tertiary: 77.7% (Table A-2). Thus, the employment and GDP ratios of each sector show that the Japanese economy is certainly concentrated in the tertiary sector from the aspects of employment and GDP.

Table A-1   Change in Japan's Employment Ratio by Sector

Research Year	1950	1970	1990	2000	2014	2016
Working People (million)	35.63	52.20	61.68	62.98	63.51	63.76
Primary Industry (%)	48.3	19.3	7.1	5.0	3.6	3.5
Secondary Industry (%)	21.7	33.9	33.0	29.2	23.8	24.1
(Manufacture)	(15.7)	(25.9)	(23.4)	(19.1)	(15.8)	(15.1)
Tertiary Industry (%)	30.0	46.8	59.9	65.8	72.6	72.3

Source: Statistics 2016, Cabinet Office, Government of Japan

Table A-2   Change in Japan's GDP Ratio by Sector

	2005	2010	2015	2016
Real GDP (trillion)	524.1	500.3	500.5	538.4
Primary Sector (%)	1.1	1.1	1.1	1.1
Secondary Sector (%)	21.5	20.8	20.4	21.0
Tertiary Sector (%)	77.4	78.1	78.4	77.7

Source: Statistics 2016, Cabinet Office, Government of Japan

2. Factors of Service Industry Shift

Based on past experience, it is widely known that the industrial structure of the economy changes along with economic development. Petty-Clark's Law is one of the main academic theories that describes this change. This Law states that as the economy develops, the weight of the economy will shift from the primary sector to the secondary sector and then to the tertiary sector. What is the reason for this shift in the industrial structure? The following four reasons have been identified.

(1) *Income Inequality Between Sectors*

As productivity begins to increase due to the industrial revolution, income inequality begins to appear between sectors. The labor force shifts between industries in pursuit of higher incomes. In the secondary sector, revolutions in manufacturing technology result in increased productivity in factories and higher incomes for labor working in these factories. On the other hand, in the primary sector, there are very few factors that would cause a dramatic expansion of production due to technological revolution. Since the primary sector concerns materials found in nature, even if revolutions in the technology used to gather these resources occur, the range over which these resources can be gathered is still limited. Therefore, income inequality arises between different sectors.

(2) *Changes in Demand Structure*

As income levels increase, consumption structure changes as well. The demand for services, rather than things, grows. Consumers start wanting to go to restaurants, go traveling, watch movies, and use smartphones. Consumers' desire for things other than material objects increases. Therefore, since developed countries already have a large amount of possessions, the weight of the economy begins to shift towards the third sector.

(3) *Globalization of Industry*

As corporations expand overseas, it is advantageous to import products produced overseas rather than produce them domestically in some situations. This results in a decrease in the proportion of the economy engaged in manufacturing industries, which make up the secondary sector, and an increase in the proportion of the economy engaged in the tertiary sector. Although many reasons exist for corporations expanding overseas, this phenomenon is caused by corporations expanding overseas in pursuit of low cost labor. It is for the same reason that there have been recent expansions of many corporations in America, Europe, and Japan into China. As a result, products "made in China" are now widely available in developed countries.

(4) *Shift Towards Services within the Manufacturing Industry*

Along with advances in technological innovation and increased sophistication and diversity of consumer demand, the proportion of workers engaged in indirect departments such as sales, research and development, design, marketing and promotion, information technology, planning, and management within the manufacturing industry has increased. This trend is referred to as the shift towards a service economy within the manufacturing industry. Although the manufacturing industry is classified as an industrial sector that produces concrete objects, in order to sell those products, this industry also needs functions such as marketing to respond to consumer demands and software development. The computer industry is one of the main examples of this. Although hardware can be mass produced due to the effects of technological innovation, software development must be done separately for each system. As a result, the number of workers engaged in this service industry is increasing. In addition, another reason for this shift is that corporations in the manufacturing industry are expanding into new business areas in the tertiary sector in order to make effective use of excess capital and excess labor. The expansion of the manufacturing industry into real estate, IT, transport, communications, financial services, and insurance is another factor that contributes to the increased shift towards a service economy.

3. Characteristics of Service Industry

Unlike the manufacturing industry, which makes tangible products such as automobiles, electronics, chemicals, foods, etc., the service industry belongs to the field of nonmanufacturing industries which basically offers intangible service such as construction, commerce, finance, insurance, communication, etc. The difference between the manufacturing industry and service industry can be perceived with the following two concepts: universality for the former, and individuality for the latter. In the manufacturing industry, standardized mass production in a plant is the norm, and in this sense, it can be regarded as universal. The service industry, on the other hand, can be understood as individual, since mass production of service is impossible due to the diversity of clients, the recipients of the service. Also, many types of business are part of the service industry, such as hotels, department stores, banks, securities companies, supermarkets, convenience stores, entertainment firms, and so on. They have something in common, in that each can be understood as an indigenous industry inseparable from its locality. In the service industry, production and consumption of services are simultaneous and inseparable from each other, unlike in the manufacturing industry where the production of goods and their consumption take place in different locations. Thus, the characteristics of the service industry can be understood from the aspects of intangibility, simultaneity, heterogeneity, nonstorability, nontransportability, as well as individuality.

Intangibility refers to functions or effects that cannot be grasped in the shape of concrete things.

Simultaneity refers to the fact that production and consumption of services are interlocked. Heterogeneity refers to the difficulty of standardization or equalization of services to be offered, since they cannot be uniformly mass-produced in factories, and to the fact that they tend to vary widely.

Nonstorability indicates the characteristic of service which cannot be prepared and stored, as can ready-made products, and thus service may vanish on the spot.

Nontransportability refers to the fact that services themselves cannot be transported from one place to another, unless the provider of the service moves.

Now that the characteristics of the service industry have been made clear, I would like to proceed by considering the main theme of this paper, that is, the globalization of the service industry, from several viewpoints.

For example, the supermarket Yaohan, which was based in Shizuoka Prefecture in Japan and originally in the distribution industry, expanded by opening up new markets in Asia, the USA, and Europe under the powerful leadership of the management of Kazuo Wada. In a further leap forward, Mr. Wada established in Shanghai, China the Shanghai Yaohan Department Store on a scale said to be the largest in the East, jointly with a local department store. Yaohan's corporate headquarters in Japan itself was moved to Hong Kong. However, behind such great international strides, Yaohan's domestic business slumped and eventually went bankrupt.

Apart from this, there are quite a few similar instances among hotels, banks, retailers, tourism companies, etc., which are part of the Japanese nonmanufacturing industry that, with the rapid rise of the yen in 1985 providing the momentum, expanded their business abroad in major cities of the world. But most of them, unlike more typical MNCs, did not intend to expand their markets to local customers, but rather to focus on expatriate Japanese residents in the relevant cities.

These activities extended by the service industry eventually had be withdrawn because of the reduction of Japanese markets owing to the stagnation of the Japanese economy from the 1990s onward. The scale of investment required to establish business outposts in the service industry is not as big as in the manufacturing industry.

Also, the former's stance is basically different from that of the latter. Companies in the manufacturing industry tend to conduct their business with a long- term outlook for a harmonious relationship with the indigenous community by establishing their production plants there. One of the reasons for the reduction or withdrawal of overseas operations once extended by the Japanese service industry is that they were often run as one-man business or a mere flight of fancy by top management, and as a result had lacked reliable feasibility studies.

4. Service Industry in Japanese MNCs

The strength of Japanese multinational corporations is in the manufacturing industry where high-quality products are made using excellent technology. In the production of automobiles, machinery, and electronics, Japanese worldwide business operations are being developed to feature their products as global brands. From the viewpoint of the research of international management, the primary object of the study of Japanese MNCs is overseas expansion of the manufacturing industry, and in particular, their system of management in the countries where they intend to open up new markets following the transfer of their production operation abroad. The reason for this is that the realities of international management motivate MNCs, and that its core stage is found in production activities abroad.

The decision about whether or not overseas production should be carried out involves the corporation's fundamental strategy for international management, since it requires a larger investment than merely establishing marketing outposts. Therefore, by establishing a production footing, MNC management activities gain importance and carry out part of the managerial strategy of its headquarters.

So, is the expansion of the service industry abroad not a true picture of MNCs? Among European and American MNCs in the service industry field, the global management policies of banks such as Citibank and HSBC, insurance companies such as American Family,

Zurich, and American Home Direct, transportation companies such as FedEx and DHL, department stores such as Robinson and Sears, convenience store such as 7-Eleven Lawson, and am/pm, theme parks such as Disney Resort and Universal Studios, computer software companies such as Microsoft and Google, and the world's largest retailer, Walmart, are familiar to us in Japan.

In light of the prosperity of these MNCs, the question arises as to why Japanese businesses are so weak in the multinationalization of the service industry.

Apart from the lack of a production footing overseas, the service industry is no different from the manufacturing industry, in that both procure local materials and sell their end products in the local market. The problem is how such activities overseas are incorporated into the managerial strategy of the corporate headquarters, and with what kind of global vision these activities are promoted. From this standpoint, it is doubtful that the overseas development of the Japanese service industry has been regarded as a keystone of corporate strategy. Like the rest of Japanese industry, the domestic market of the service industry is now reaching its peak due to the decrease in Japan's population of young people as well as its aging population. Further growth in the Japanese service industry cannot be expected unless the sphere of activity is expanded abroad. The globalization of the service industry is a strategic issue that influences the industrial policies of the 21st century.

5. Why the Japanese Service Industry Lacks International Competitiveness?

Why has the Japanese service industry failed to be highly competitive internationally? Let us consider some of the primary factors.

(1) *Particularistic Management*

The factor to be considered first is the international transferability of Japanese management. The transfer of technology from the

Japanese manufacturing industry, whose superiority in production technology is its source of worldwide competitiveness, mainly takes place in developing counties. But how about management expertise? In the past, features such as lifetime employment, a seniority system, or an in-house union shone throughout the world as positive characteristics of Japanese management. But these features may be mere eccentricities, especially when compared with the American form of management. Yohtaro Yoshino, professor at the Harvard Business School, observed these characteristics of Japanese management and termed them 'particularistic.' From the global viewpoint, the Japanese form of management is quite distinct, and consequently, to transfer abroad is not easy.

American management, on the other hand, is 'universalistic.' In fact, much American management expertise was introduced into Japan after World War II, and diffused in a generalized form. The American service industries prospering in Japan typically disseminate their management expertise in the form of manuals. Historically, the USA had lagged behind Europe, and therefore, rapid industrialization was urgently required. In order to overcome this challenge, they had to work out a pragmatic scheme, and the expertise required for this became the central theme of their management. Since the purpose of management is to achieve objectives by organizing people, the composition of employees is a matter of great importance.

(2) *Protectionism Under the Government*

The growth of productivity in the service industry in most advanced countries is less than that in their manufacturing industry. This tendency is particularly evident in Japan; the growth of productivity in its manufacturing industry is 4.1%, whereas in the service industry it is only 0.8% (Table A-3). The primary factor relating to the internationally high competitiveness of the Japanese manufacturing industry is that the rate of growth of labor productivity is higher than in other advanced countries.

Table A-3   The Growth Rate of Labor Productivity

	USA	UK	Germany	Japan
Manufacturing	3.3%	2.0%	1.7%	4.1%
Nonmanufacturing	2.3%	1.3%	0.9%	0.8%

Source: Japan R&D Expenditure in Service Industry 2005, The Ministry of Economy, Trade and Industry

This seems to be the result of the unremitting efforts made by Japanese enterprises to raise quality control and improve productivity at their factories. The low growth of the Japanese service industry is attributable to the fact that this category of industry includes many types of businesses which have not yet been exposed to global competition.

The primary reason for this is that after World War II, the Japanese government introduced protective regulation for the service industry, closely connected as it was with the home market, so that it could avoid competition from overseas countries. For example, the Ministry of Finance, which was aiming to stabilize finance, avoided bankruptcies of financial firms by adopting a 'convoy' ('circling the wagons') policy and gave administrative guidance to financial circles for their stable management; the government also passed the Large-scale Retail Law to control the entry of large stores, particularly from abroad, in order to protect local retailers.

Productivity increases by being exposed to competition, while protective policies tend to reduce it. Continuous innovation is indispensable for the improvement of productivity, whether in the manufacturing industry or in the service industry. Regarding R&D expenditure as indispensable, the Japanese manufacturing industry has consistently invested in R&D to increase production as well as develop new products and technology. Even after the bursting of the bubble, the Japanese manufacturing industry coherently continued to invest in R&D expenditure, which has become a source of strong international competitiveness in the current Japanese manufacturing industry.

Table A-4   Percentage of R&D Expenditure in
Manufacturing Industry and Nonmanufacturing
Industry

	USA	Japan
Manufacturing	57%	88%
Nonmanufacturing	43%	12%

Source: The Ministry of Economy, Trade and Industry,
2005

What about the service industry? Table A-4 show a comparison between the USA and Japan concerning R&D expenditures paid by the manufacturing industry and the nonmanufacturing industry. In the USA, the ratio of R&D expenditure paid by the manufacturing industry is almost the same as that by the nonmanufacturing industry; in Japan, however, the ratio paid by the manufacturing industry is much higher than that by the nonmanufacturing industry.

6. Overseas Expansion of Familiar Service Industries

In recent years, there has been a notable trend towards overseas expansion of non-manufacturing service industries. In this section, we introduce several examples that the reader will probably be familiar with and discuss overseas expansion of these industries.

(1) *Japanese Restaurants*

In the past, it was often said that Japanese companies in the ser vice industry were not competitive compared to similar corporations from Europe and America when expanding overseas.

Several examples of American food service companies that are familiar to most consumers include McDonald's, KFC, Mister Donut, and Starbucks in recent years. These companies have grown to become global brands and have store locations everywhere around the world.

Table A-5   Overseas Expansion of Japanese Restaurants

	Number in Japan	Number Outside Japan
CoCo Ichibanya Curry	1.296	161
Saizeriya Italian	1.028	345
MOS Burger	1.359	333
Ootoya Japanese Food	342	94
Saboten Tonkatsu	300	94
Yoshinoya Meat Bowl	2.328	780
Genki Sushi	136	117
Ajisen Ramen	86	677
Ippudo	125	63

In recent years, there are several companies operating Japanese restaurants that are expanding their businesses overseas, although the size of these companies is still small compared to their American counterparts. Table A-5 shows the number of store locations of restaurants expanding overseas as of 2017.

One of the most well-known types of Japanese food is sushi. Sushi is one of the highlights of Japanese food culture when introducing Japanese culture to foreigners. Originally, sushi was prepared by sushi chefs who made sushi for each individual customer. Sushi was one of the more expensive types of Japanese cuisine, and was not something that common people could eat every day. 'Kaiten sushi' (conveyor belt sushi) has turned sushi into food that is easily available to the common people by serving sushi to customers on conveyor belts, similar to a factory. Some of the largest conveyor belt sushi restaurants include Sushiro, Kappa Sushi, and Kura Sushi. Japanese sushi based on the conveyor belt concept has expanded to Asia, America, and even the Middle East.

Now, sushi is no longer something that belongs only to the Japanese. British entrepreneur Simon Woodroffe opened "YO! Sushi" in London based on the Japanese conveyor belt sushi model. YO! Sushi has over 70 locations in the UK, and is expanding to several countries in Europe and the Middle East. The invention of

Table A-6   Conveyor Belt Sushi Restaurants in Asia

Japan	1.050	Sushiro, Kappa, Kura, Genki Sushi
Taiwan	200	Sushi Express (Taiwan Owner)
Hong Kong	50	Genki Sushi
China	173	Genki Sushi, Sushi Express (Taiwan Owner)
Malaysia	70	Sushi King
South Korea	38	Sushiro, Kappa, Sushi Hiroba

sushi restaurants using conveyor belts has made it possible for Japan's sushi culture to spread around the world, even without the presence of sushi chefs. Currently, sushi restaurants in Japan are engaged in fierce competition, and are searching for growth through overseas expansion. In addition, the recent economic growth in Asia has also resulted in the boom of Japanese food, and many conveyor belt sushi restaurants are opening store locations there. See Table A-6. Japanese cuisine was also registered as a UNESCO Intangible Cultural Heritage in 2015. Hence, Japanese restaurants are expanding in Asia at an even faster pace than they are expanding in America.

(2) *Overseas Strategies of Unique Companies*

Several brands with unique products from Japan that are rapidly expanding overseas include Uniqlo, Mujirushi Ryohin (Muji), Daiso, Kumon, Benesse, Yamato Transport, Nitori, and Nintendo. We focus on the examples of Muji and Uniqlo, which are two brands that are particularly familiar to many consumers, and also on 7-Eleven.

Muji

Ryohin Keikaku Co., Ltd. operates under the brand name of Mujirushi Ryohin in Japan, and as Muji overseas. This company began as a private brand of Seiyu in 1980, and offered only 40 products in the beginning. Currently, Muji carries over 4,000 products, including food, apparel, and even electronic appliances. Muji expands its customer base through its unique strategy of offering simplified versions of products needed in daily life and promoting a lifestyle that values functionality. Ryohin Keikaku currently operates 344 stores in 20 countries around the world.

Previously, the retail industry for household items was dominated by local companies who were more familiar with the local culture and needs. It was believed that this was a domestic industry that was hard for foreign companies to enter. However, Ryohin Keikaku continued their strategy of offering a new lifestyle in overseas markets and recognized that consumers overseas also shared the mentality of valuing simplicity and functionality in household products even though their cultures were different. In this way, Muji overcame problems faced by many brands previously, and was able to increase the number of overseas stores they operated. It could be said that this company has a product sense that is different from Japanese culture right from the beginning.

In Muji's first efforts at overseas expansion, Muji worked towards opening stores in top locations in large cities in European countries with conservative historical cultures, including the UK, France, and Italy. However, the stores were not successful in the beginning. Muji bravely moved forward while overcoming many challenges. As a result, Muji now directly operates 312 stores in Japan, supplies products to 102 stores, and operates 344 stores overseas. These figures reveal that the number of Muji overseas stores is greater than the number of directly operated stores in Japan. In particular, Muji has 160 stores in China, which demonstrates the popularity of the Muji brand in this country and also reveals Muji's efforts at expansion in this country. Muji expanded its logistics center in Shanghai in 2013 in order to improve its shipping systems overseas, improved their ability to procure raw materials in a timely manner, and lowered the cost of procurement through streamlining logistics.

Mujirushi Ryohin's strength is in the lifestyle that they promote. Mujirushi Ryohin focuses on their philosophy of providing feel-good living at a reasonable price and considering matters from the perspective of manufacturing (selecting materials, inspecting processes, and simplifying packaging) throughout their product development process.

Uniqlo

Uniqlo's brand name comes from the phrase 'Unique Clothing Warehouse.' Uniqlo's headquarters are located in Yamaguchi prefecture. Their company name is Fast Retailing. Tadashi Yanai, the current director, took over a retail store for women's apparel, and transformed it into a global brand that rivals brands such as Spain's Zara and Sweden's H&M in the apparel manufacturing and retail industry (specialty store retailer of private label apparel, or SPA) through his strong leadership.

Uniqlo's sales for 2016 totaled 1,455.2 billion yen (domestic sales: 799.8 billion yen, overseas sales: 655.4 billion yen). The number of domestic stores was 837, and the number of overseas stores was 958. The number of overseas stores is larger. Since the domestic market is anticipated to be affected by the declining birthrate, aging population, and decreasing population, Uniqlo is counting on the overseas markets. Therefore, Uniqlo focuses on the overseas market. Although overseas sales accounted for only 10% of total sales in 2010, overseas sales account for almost half of total sales currently.

For Japanese manufacturing global brands such as Canon and Sony, overseas sales currently make up almost two-thirds of their total sales. However, these companies have a long history of overseas expansion which extends for over half a century. On the other hand, Uniqlo increased their overseas sales to almost half of their total sales in the short time span of only several decades. Uniqlo is considered as a pioneering brand that demonstrates the international competitiveness of the Japanese service industry.

Previously, the casual wear fashion category was dominated by brands from Europe and America. It was considered taboo for an Asian company to become a global brand in this category. Although Uniqlo's first expansion overseas was to the UK in 2002, it was not widely known back then and was not successful. However, Yanai strongly believed that in the world of apparel, brands should become established in Europe and America first before they could expand globally. Based on his beliefs, Yanai opened large-scale flagship stores in prime locations in large global cities such as London, Paris, New York, and Shanghai, and attempted to transform Uniqlo into a global brand.

Uniqlo now intends to increase their proportion of overseas sales to around 70% to 80% of total sales and increase their overseas sales total by a factor of 50 to between 3.5 trillion yen to 4 trillion yen in the next 10 years. Although brands such as Zara and H&M are popular in Europe and America, it is anticipated that the brand that enjoys the most popularity in the growing countries of Asia and China will be Uniqlo from Japan. Guided by the grand vision of the founder Yanai that was captured in the slogan 'Change clothes, change conventional wisdom, change the world,' Uniqlo has succeeded in expanding their business by bringing out latent demand among customers and creating many hit products. Uniqlo's products are not cheap and low quality. Uniqlo develops products according to its product strategy which focuses on customer satisfaction through focusing on quality at a reasonable cost. Uniqlo has a thorough quality control system and employs long-term strategic cooperation with its factories operated by Chinese companies.

7-Eleven

During the second half of the 19th century in the United States, the widespread application of mass-production techniques associated with the Second Industrial Revolution was accompanied by a revolution, with the introduction of chain stores and urban department stores. Unlike older kinds of stores, these new types of retailers looked for large sales volumes at low margins.

The convenience store can be dated from the early 20th century. Southland, founded in 1927, claims to have been the world's first convenience store chain. Southland's success had been facilitated by favorable market conditions. Large self-service supermarkets had been introduced in the United States in the 1930s, but their growth had been constrained first by economic depression and then by wartime restrictions. From the 1950s, supermarkets began to rapidly drive neighborhood mom-and-pop stores out of business. This trend accelerated in the 1960s, providing a niche for the convenience store, who could serve customers in a hurry who wished to buy only a few items. Southland and other convenience chains exploited this niche by locating their stores near residential areas, more often in fast growing suburbs than in urban centers. By lengthening their hours of operation, sometimes to 24 hours, convenience stores further differentiated themselves from supermarkets.

The convenience store industry in the United States was successful in the 1970s and early 1980s, but began to falter in the late 1980s and early 1990s. In the late 1980s, major oil companies, accustomed to the rigors of intense competition, entered the market. Competition was intense, and many retailers borrowed excessively to expand and diversify. As a result, 14 convenience store companies filed for bankruptcy from 1989 to 1991.

In early 1990, Southland's sales began sagging, due to a shortage of funds to reposition and refurbish its stores, competition from emerging regional chains, and an inability to come to terms with changing trends and consumer demand in the retail business.

On March 5, 1991, after five months in bankruptcy, Southland Corporation was acquired by Ito-Yokado, the extremely successful licensee of 7-Eleven stores in Japan since 1973. The deal involved the purchase of 70% of Southland for US$430 million by IYG Holding Co., wholly owned by Ito-Yokado Co. Ltd. and 7-Eleven Japan Co. Ltd. The purchase gave Ito-Yokado control of more than 7,000 American and Canadian stores as well as franchise authority in 20 other countries.

Southland decided to learn from its new Japanese owner, and embarked on a radical new campaign: a shift in focus from the historical emphasis on volume sales to an emphasis on customer satisfaction. Southland's strategy (heavily influenced by Ito-Yokado) focused primarily on three key areas: pricing, store remodeling and remerchandising, and inventory management/new product development.

Specifically, Southland chose to change the pricing strategy, by turning away from heavy discounting of merchandise and to focus instead on selling products at an 'everyday fair price.' This new pricing policy contrasted strongly with Southland's former practice of heavily discounting merchandise to attract customers.

Another key area strategy was the remodeling and remerchandising of 7-Eleven stores. The store remodeling involved a general facelift: lower shelves, new in-store signs, better lighting and decluttering of the sales counter. Remerchandising involved the addition of a wide variety of new products, such as fresh foods, staples in preferred sizes, and more upscale offerings.

Also, one of the most important changes involved distribution management. The key to Ito-Yokado's success with 7-Eleven Japan had been the use of its inventory and physical distribution management systems that resulted in lower on-hand inventory, faster inventory turnover and, most importantly, accurate information on customer buying habits.

Table A-7   Expansion of Convenience Stores in the Asian Market

	Thailand	Philippine	Malaysia	Singapore	Indonesia	Vietnam
7-Eleven	8.832	1.602	1.944	458	187	0
Lawson	42	12	0	0	38	0
Family Mart	109	108	0	0	27	87
Ministop	517	0	0	0	6	31

Source: Japan Economic News paper, March 27, 2016

Table A-8   Number of 7-Eleven Stores Worldwide

	End of March, 2008	End of March, 2014	End of March, 2017
Japan	12.006	16.375	19.171
America	8.563	8.163	8.563
Thailand	4.402	7.651	9.542
Korea	1.802	7.000	8.556
Taiwan	4.770	4.996	5.107

Table A-8   (*Continued*)

	End of March, 2008	End of March, 2014	End of March, 2017
China	1.381	2.010	2.357
Mexico	826	1.899	1.878
Malaysia	909	1.581	2.122
Philippine	318	1.049	1.995
Australia	363	596	646
Singapore	419	528	417
Indonesia	0	158	155
World	34.147	52.811	61.554

Source: Japan Economic News paper, August 2, 2016

7. Outlook for the Japanese Service Industry

Lastly, we describe the characteristics of the Japanese service industry, and provide an analysis of the industry from several different perspectives.

(1) *Targeting Asia*

An examination of the history of the globalization of Japanese companies reveals that trading companies were some of the earliest pioneers in the pre-war era. Manufacturing companies looked towards Europe and America for the basis for their products, increased their international competitiveness by applying Japan's advanced manufacturing technology, and developed along a path that took them from exports to overseas sales and finally to overseas production. Overseas markets at that time mainly consisted of the markets of developed countries, where European and American companies earned foreign currency through trading in these countries, which contributed to the growth of the Japanese economy.

However, the main overseas market of the service industry has shifted to Asia and China in recent years. In these regions, Japanese products are highly trusted, due to the reputation that Japanese brands have built up in the manufacturing industry. Furthermore, growing income levels in these regions as a result of economic growth have also created growing markets for service industries. As income levels rise, consumers' interest towards food and apparel also increase, resulting in an increased number of consumers going out to eat Japanese food, going shopping at Uniqlo, and making purchases at convenience stores, thereby resulting in heightened levels of consumer demand for daily necessities. As shown in this chapter, Japanese sushi restaurants and convenience stores all anticipate that the Asian and Chinese markets will continue to grow in the future.

(2) *Entrepreneurial Spirit*

Many companies in the Japanese service industry started as family-operated companies, and so many of these companies lack the financial clout of their manufacturing counterparts. While many manufacturing companies founded by individuals in the post-war era and former Zaibatsu (Japanese business conglomerates) companies grew through restructuring and were early in expanding overseas, the service industry had always been a domestic industry, was not aggressive in pursuing overseas expansion, and focused on expanding their business in the domestic market. However, as the brand reputation of Japanese manufacturers continues to grow overseas, entrepreneurial-minded individuals interested in expanding their business overseas have also begun to emerge in the service industry as well. While entrepreneurs interested in expanding their business overseas first began to emerge in the 1970s in the manufacturing industry, the new generations of entrepreneurs did not emerge in the service industry until the 2000s. Overseas expansions of Japanese restaurants, sushi restaurants, and ramen restaurants became possible due to the presence of leaders, such as Uniqlo's Tadashi Yanai, Rakuten's Hiroshi Mikitani, Softbank's Masayoshi Son, and Ryohin Keikaku's Tadamitsu Matsui. Overseas business are inherently risky endeavors. Success is not possible without the brave efforts that are born from an entrepreneurial spirit. The necessity of a global mindset amongst the management is a qualitative feature of multinational companies that is pointed out earlier in this paper.

(3) *Accumulation of Management Knowledge*

During the 1980s when overseas expansion of manufacturing companies was in full swing, there were several examples of service industries that also expanded overseas. A small number of companies such as hotels operated by airlines, department stores, banks, and securities companies did expand overseas. However, their customers were mainly local subsidiaries and Japanese companies, and these companies did not succeed in fully entering the local markets.

However, recent overseas expansions by companies in the service industry are proving to be successful in the local markets. These companies are considering long-term growth through strategic global management. One factor of this phenomenon is the accumulation of management knowledge. Since the Japanese service industry grew while it was focused on the domestic market, the amount of management knowledge accumulated by these companies that is applicable overseas is limited compared to manufacturers. For example, the strength of American service industry companies lies in the accumulation of knowledge in universal management manuals, which is the essence of American management. Conversely, Japanese service industry companies operate in a society that relies on unspoken understandings between Japanese people, which makes it difficult to transfer management knowledge to overseas branches. However, as American and European service industry companies began to expand to Japan, Japanese service industry companies also began to adopt efficient management through the use of manuals. The accumulation of management methods that also apply overseas while preserving a Japanese-style spirit of service is a factor that contributes to the recent overseas expansion of the Japanese service industry.

(4) *Expansion through M&A*

In this section, we have introduced several examples of overseas expansion by service industry companies familiar to most consumers. However, other large companies such as banks, securities companies, insurance companies, and information and communications companies are also actively expanding overseas. Previously, these companies expanded mainly through operation bases in major cities in Europe, America, Asia, and China, but companies have also began to expand overseas through the use of M&A in recent years.

The increase in overseas expansions through M&A has been explained in Chapter 2. M&A by companies in the service industry are growing in terms of both the amount of money and the number of cases. Before, the service industry was considered as a domestic industry, and growth happened gradually through the expansion of the domestic market. However, due to the aging population and rapid maturation of domestic economic activities, companies have been forced to look for growth opportunities overseas. In this case, rather than developing overseas markets one step at a time through the application of a green field investment strategy which had been applied before, companies can gain faster access to local markets and synergistic effects by purchasing existing companies. Therefore, companies with large amounts of capital such as banks, insurance companies, securities companies, and information and communications companies are accelerating their rate of overseas expansions through the use of M&A.

(5) *Securing Human Resources*

In the service industry in Japan, there is a history of family-operated companies growing within the domestic market and expanding overseas later on. However, family-operated companies placed too much focus on the domestic market and failed to systematically nurture human resources for managing overseas businesses. However, these companies have begun to send their children overseas to study and gain overseas management experience in response to the trend towards globalization by the second and third generations, and systematically nurture human resources with a global mindset. One reason for this is that these companies have realized that it is necessary to nurture global human resources in order to expand to overseas markets amidst a maturing domestic market in the future.

Today, the increasingly inward-focused nature of university students is considered a problem. It is necessary to examine this trend one student at a time. In other words, it is untrue to state that everyone in the younger generation does not want to go overseas. Rather, there are still many students who want to study abroad, work abroad, or work in international organizations. Overall, the number of people who have studied abroad, lived abroad, or grew up abroad is increasing. There are many young people who dream of working overseas and want to work in a position with overseas contact.

In addition, the number of overseas students, from Asia and China in particular, studying in Japan has reached a significant number. These students serve as bridges linking Japan and their countries once they return to their home countries. In the past, growth of Japanese companies was due to the creation of global brands in the manufacturing industry. Companies are now inviting international students from abroad to contribute to the nurturing of foreign human resources who can lead overseas expansion of companies in the service industry.

This chapter was first published in the Review of Business Administration Vol. 42, No. 2 by Soka University in 2018.

References

Aguilar, F. J. 1994. *Managing Corporate Ethics: Learning from America's Ethical Companies How to Supercharge Business Performance.* Oxford University Press.

Asakawa, K. 1996. External-Internal Linkage and Overseas Autonomy-Control Tension: The Management Dilemma of Japanese R&D in Europe. *IEEE Transaction on Engineering Management*, Vol. 43, No. 1.

Asakawa, K., and Lehrer, M. 2003. Managing Local Knowledge Asset Globally: The Role of Regional Innovation Relays. *Journal of World Business*, Vol. 38, No. 1.

Aharoni, Y., and Nachum, L. (2000) "Globalization of Service", Routledge.

Anthony, G., and Makino, S. (2007) "Multinational Corporation in the Service Sector: A Strategy of Japanese Trading Companies," Journal of International Business Studies, Vol. 38.

Bartlett, C., and Ghoshal, S. 1989. *Managing Across Borders: The Transnational Solution.* Harvard Business School Press.

Bartlett, C., and Ghoshal, S. 1990. Managing Innovation in the Transnational Corporation. In *Managing the Global Firm*, edited by C. Bartlett, Y. Doz, and G. Hedlund. Routledge.

Bartlett, C., Doz, Y., and Hedlund, G. eds. 1990. *Managing the Global Firm.* Routledge.

Boddewyn, J. J., and Perry, A. C. (1986) "Service Multinationals: Conceptualization, Measurement and Theory," Journal of International Business Studies, Vol. 17, Issue 3.

Bouttller, R., Gassmann, O., and von Zedwitz, M. 2008. *Managing Global Innovation: Uncovering the Secrets of Future Competitiveness.* Springer.

Breiding, R. J. 2013. *Swiss Made: The Untold Story Behind Switzerland's Success*. Profile Books.

Camphell, A. J., and Kerbeke, A. (1994) "The Globalization of Service Multinationals," Long Range Planning, Vol. 27, No. 2.

Cantwell, J. 1989. *Technological Innovation and Multinational Corporations*. Basil Blackwell.

Casson, M., ed. 1991. *Global Research Strategy and International Competitiveness*. Blackwell.

Cheng, J. L., and Bolon, D. 1993. The Management of Multinational R&D: A Neglected Topic in International Business Research. *Journal of International Business Studies*, Vol. 24.

Christopher, H., and Yip, G. (1986) "Developing Global Strategies for Service Business," California Management Review, Vol. 38, No. 2.

Deal, T. E., and Kennedy, A. A. 1982. *Corporate Cultures: The Rites and Rituals of Corporate Life*. Addison-Wesley.

De George, R. 1993. *Competing with Integrity in International Business*. Oxford University Press.

DeMeyer, A., and Mizushima, A. 1989. Global R&D Management. *R&D Management*, Vol. 19, No. 2.

DeMeyer, A. 1993. Management of an International Network of Industrial R&D Laboratories. *R&D Management*, Vol. 23, No. 2.

Donaldson, T. 1989. *The Ethics of International Business*. Oxford University Press.

Dunning, J. H. (1989) "Multinational Enterprise and Growth of Service: Some Conceptual and Theoretical Issues" Service Industries Journal, Vol. 9, No. 1.

Dunning. J. H. (1989) "Transnational Corporation and Growth of Service, Some Conceptual and Theoretical Issues" United Nations, New York.

Dunning, J. H. (1990) "The Internationalization of Production of Service: Some General and Specific Explanations" AIB Annual Conference, Toronto.

Dymsza, W. 1972. *Multinational Business Strategy*. McGraw-Hill.

Enatsu, K., Ohtowa, T., and Fujisawa, T. (2008) "Service Sangyo no Kokusaitenkai" (International Management of Service Industries), Cyuoh Keizaisha.

Hall, E. (1976) "Beyond Culture," Macmillan.

Hall, E. T. 1976. *Beyond Culture*. Anchor Press/Doubleday.

Heenan, D. A., and Perlmutter, H. V. 1979. *Multinational Organization Development*. Addison-Wesley.

Helmut, H. 1994. My Personal History as Nestlé CEO. *Japan Economic Newspaper*, September 1–30.

Imanishi, T. (2001) "Ryokougyou no Kokusaikeiei" (International Management of Travel Business), Koyo Shobo.

Ito, Y., and Tanaka, Y. 2014. Localization of Business Model. *International Business Review* (Japan Academy of International Business), Vol. 6, No. 2.

Jeffery, R. B. (2005) "7-Eleven in America and Japan," in Creating Modern Capitalism. Thomas, K. McCraw. Ed., Harvard Business School Press.

Kawabata, M. (2003) "Kourigyo no Kaigaishinsyutsu" (Overseas Strategy of Retail Business).

Kotabe, M. (1995) "The Return of 7-Eleven from Japan; the Vanguard Program," Columbia Journal of World Business, Winter 1995.

Kurosawa, T. 2010. Europe Multinationals and Nationalism: Case of Nestlé, La Roche, Unilever. *Business Review* (Kobe University), Vol. 202, No. 5.

Kurosawa, T. 2012. Multinational Organization of La Roche Switzerland. *Economic Review* (Hiroshima University), Vol. 36, No. 2.

Li, J., and Guisinger, S. (1992) "The Globalization of Service Multinationals in the Triad Region: Japan," Western Europe and North America," Journal of International Business Studies 23, Fourth Quarter.

Merchant, H., and Gaur, A. (2008) "Opening the Non-Manufacturings Envelope: The Next Big Enterprise for International Business Research," Management International Review, Vol. 48.

Nakamura, H., and Gaur, A. (2003) "Theory for Global Retail Business," Japan Academy of International Business.

Nakatani, I. (1987) "Changing the Japanese Corporation," Kodansha.

Nishi, S. (2002) "Globalization of Consulting Firm," Kobe University of Commerce.

Nestlé Compensation Report. 2017, 2018.

Nestlé Corporate Governance Report. 2017, 2018.

Nestlé Financial Statement. 2017, 2018.

Nestlé Business Case. Keio Business School, 2004.

Nestlé Code of Conduct. https://www.nestle.co.jp/asset-library/document/about-us/2017

Nestlé Corporate Business Principles. https://www.nestle.com/sites/default/files/asset-library/documents/library/documents/corporate_governance/corporate-business-principles-en.pdf

Nonaka, I., and Takeuchi, H. 1995. *The Knowledge Creation Company.* Oxford University Press.

Oh, Lin. (2008) "Nippon no Kourigyo no Kyosouryoku," (Compeitiveness of Japanese Retail Business — Practice of Ito Yokado Super Market in China), Hitotsubashi Business Review.

Peters, T. J., and Waterman, R. H. 1972. *In Search of Excellence.* Harper & Row.

Pfiffner, A. 2014. *Henri Nestlé 1814–1890: From Pharmacist's Assistant to Founder of the World's Leading Nutrition, Health and Wellness Company.* Nestlé.

Pfiffner, A. 1995. *Henri Nestlé: Vom Frankfurter Apothekergehilfen zum Schweizer Pionierunternehmer; 1814–1890.* Nestlé.

Pfiffner, A., Renk, H., and Fenner, T. 2016. *Nestlé 150 Years: Nutrition, Health, and Wellness, 1866–2016.* Editions du Chene.

Porter, M. E., and Kramer, M. R. 2006. Strategy and Society: The Link between Competitive Advantage and Corporate Social Responsibility. *Harvard Business Review*, Vol. 84, No. 12.

Sauvant, K. P., and Mallampally, P. (1993) "Transnational Corporation in Service," Routledge.

Sawa, T. (1990) "Introduction of Service Economy," Chikurasyobou.

Schwarz, F. 2010. *Peter Brabeck-Letmathe and Nestlé — A Portrait: Creating Shared Value.* Stämpfli.

Shinomiya, Y. (1996) "Practice of Japanese Hotel Business," Kobe University of Commerce.

Takahashi, H. (2012) "The Challenge for Japanese Multinationals," Palgrave Macmillan. Takahashi, H. (2017) "International Management," Dobunkan Shuppan.

Takahashi, H. 2013. *The Challenge for Japanese Multinationals: Strategic Issues for Global Management.* Palgrave Macmillan.

Takahashi, H. 1986. Top Management System of Japanese Corporations through International Comparison. *Business Review* (Chuo University), Vol. 11 (Japanese).

Takahashi, H. 1984. Organization of European & American Multinational Corporations' Business Research. Business Research Institute, Tokyo (Japanese).

Takahashi, H. 2019. Nestlé Management. *Hakuoh Business Review,* Vol. 24, No. 2.

Takahashi, H. 1989. RHQs of Japanese MNCs. *Nihon Keizai Shimbun*, April, 24 (Japanese).

Takahashi, H. 1999. R&D Siting in Silicon Valley. *Hakuoh Business Review*, Vol. 6, March.

Tishe, N. M. 1987. *Transformational Leadership*. Prentice-Hall.

Toyoda, M. (2006) "Aiming at the Reformation of the Service Industries," Hitotsubashi Business Review.

Umasaka, T. (2003) "Process of International Retail," Hosei University.

Ushio, J. (2007) "Service Unit of Japanese Industry," Ministry of Economy Trade and Industry, April.

Vernon, R. 1971. *Sovereignty at Bay; The Multinational Spread of US Enterprises*. Basic Books.

Yoshihara, H. (2001) "International Management," Yuhikaku.

Yoshimori, M. 1976. Conception and Behavior of Western Business. Diamond, Tokyo (Japanese).

Yoshimori, M. 1984. Conception and Behavior of French Business. Diamond, Tokyo (Japanese).

Yoshimori, M. 2015. Conception and Behavior of German Business. Diamond, Tokyo (Japanese).

Yoshino, Y. (1977) "Japanese Multinationals," Diamond.

Interviews

At Nestlé Corporate Headquarter, Vevey, Switzerland
Mr. Michael Briner, Zone AOA (Asia, Oceania and sub-Saharan Africa) Group, Vice President
Mr. Chris Hogg, Zone AOA, Head of Corporate Communication
Ms. Claude Schwitiz, AOA, Head of Corporate Communication
Ms. Yao Yang, AOA, Beverage Strategic Business Unit
Mr. Andrew-Hartford Smith, Director, Corporate Training & Learning

At Nestlé Japan, Kobe, Japan
Mr. Kozo Takaoka, President, Nestlé Japan
Ms. Miki Kano, Executive Officer, Corporate Communication
Mr. Yuji Serizawa, Executive Officer, Human Resource
Mr. Makoto Nakaoka, Executive Officer, Marketing Management

www.ingramcontent.com/pod-product-compliance
Lightning Source LLC
Chambersburg PA
CBHW050630190326
41458CB00008B/2207